Franz Rudolf Knubel
... zur kleinsten Schar / ...with a chosen few
In memoriam Mildred Harnack-Fish

Franz Rudolf Knubel

... zur kleinsten Schar / ...with a chosen few

In memoriam Mildred Harnack-Fish

Herausgegeben von der Gedenkstätte Deutscher Widerstand
Berlin 2007

Dank With thanks to

Prof. Dr. h. c. Berthold Beitz, Alfried Krupp von Bohlen und Halbach-Stiftung, Essen
Dr. Henning Osthues-Albrecht, Sparkasse der Stadt Essen
Direktorin Christina Reich, Lehrer und Schüler der Mildred-Harnack-Oberschule
in Berlin-Lichtenberg

Zum Geleit

Mit seiner Dokumentation ihres Lebenswegs präsentiert Franz Rudolf Knubel eine eindrückliche und einfühlsame Hommage an Mildred Harnack. Wegen ihrer Teilnahme am Widerstand der „Roten Kapelle" wurde sie am 16. Februar 1943 vom NS-Regime hingerichtet, nachdem Adolf Hitler die zuvor verhängte Zuchthausstrafe aufgehoben und ein Todesurteil verlangt hatte.

Als Gattin Arvid Harnacks stand Mildred im Mittelpunkt des Widerstandskreises, den die Gestapo unter dem irreführenden Namen Rote Kapelle zusammenfasste. Ihm gehörte eine große Zahl von Oppositionellen, darunter zahlreiche Frauen, an, und er hatte einen regionalen Schwerpunkt im Raum Berlin. Der Widerstandskreis entstand schon seit der Mitte der 1930er Jahre, besaß später lockere Verbindungen zu Repräsentanten der Bewegung des 20. Juli und verfügte über weitreichende Beziehungen zum NS-Regierungsapparat.

Ähnlich wie beim Kreisauer Kreis kam es zu allerdings nicht mehr ausgereiften Bemühungen, ein Konzept für ein nach dem Zusammenbruch des Nationalsozialismus zu schaffendes Deutschland zu schaffen und sich dabei nicht zuletzt mit der Sowjetunion zu arrangieren. Schon vor dem deutschen Angriff auf die Sowjetunion bestanden Kontakte zur sowjetischen Handelsvertretung und Botschaft in Berlin, die 1941 konspirativen Charakter annahmen. Über Harnack knüpften sich jedoch zugleich enge Beziehungen zu amerikanischen Diplomaten, die jedoch im Dezember 1941 abbrachen und lange unbekannt blieben. In nur zum Teil erhalten gebliebenen Flugschriften setzte sich der engere Kern der Gruppe für eine Beendigung des

Preface

Mildred Harnack's life and fate are documented here in an impressive and sensitive homage by Franz Rudolf Knubel. Mildred Harnack was executed by the Nazi regime on February 16, 1943 for her involvement in the "Red Orchestra" resistance group. Adolf Hitler had revoked her earlier sentence of penal servitude and demanded the death sentence for her.

Mildred, the wife of Arvid Harnack, was at the center of the resistance group that the Gestapo misleadingly dubbed the "Red Orchestra." The group comprised a considerable number of opponents of the Nazis, including many women. Based in the Berlin area, it had been in existence from the mid-1930s on. It had informal contact with representatives of the movement that tried to overthrow Hitler on July 20, 1944, and wide-ranging connections with Nazi government institutions.

However, the Red Orchestra, like the Kreisau Circle, tried but was unable to fully develop a concept for the future of Germany after the collapse of National Socialism and—not least— to find a way for Germany to reach agreement with the Soviet Union. Even before Germany attacked the Soviet Union, the group was in contact with the Soviet trade mission and embassy in Berlin; in 1941 this assumed a conspiratorial aspect. Through Harnack there were also close connections with United States diplomats, but these were broken off in December 1941 and remained hidden for a long period. The inner circle of the group produced leaflets that have survived only in part. They advocated an end to the war and protested against the Nazi crimes of violence in the Soviet Union and the disastrous effects of the Russian military campaign, which had sunk into futility after the early victories.

Franz Rudolf Knubel

Krieges ein, protestierte gegen die nationalsozialistischen Gewaltverbrechen in der Sowjetunion und die verheerenden Auswirkungen des nach den ersten Anfangserfolgen militärisch aussichtslos gewordenen Russlandfeldzuges.

Der Kreis vermied hingegen eine organisatorische Verbindung zur illegalen KPD. Harro Schulze-Boysen und Arvid Harnack schwebte die Schaffung einer parteiübergreifenden Sammlungsbewegung und eine Unterwanderung nationalsozialistischer Institutionen mit dem Fernziel vor, eine klassengelöste neue Gesellschaft in Anknüpfung an Ideen der Jugendbewegung ins Leben zu rufen.

Die weitgehend scheiternden Versuche, eine Nachrichtenverbindung zur Sowjetunion aufzubauen, die schließlich zum Auffliegen der Kontakte und zu umfassenden Verhaftungsaktionen durch die Gestapo führten, standen keineswegs im Vordergrund der Widerstandstätigkeit des Kreises. Das in der frühen Bundesrepublik entstandene Bild einer kommunistischen Spionageorganisation war ein Reflex des Kalten Krieges, auch wenn es zum Informationsaustausch mit sowjetischen Verbindungsmännern noch vor dem Juni 1941 kam.

Im Mittelpunkt der von Franz Rudolf Knubel geschaffenen Ausstellung steht die in den USA geborene Hochschuldozentin Mildred Harnack. Sie repräsentiert die Weltoffenheit wie die Verankerung des überwiegend der oberen Mittelschicht angehörenden Widerstandskreises in der deutschen idealistischen Bildungstradition. Während sie zum einen über ihre Kontakte zur US-Botschaft außenpolitische Informationen beschaffte, unterstützte sie die illegale Arbeit und war vor allem im Zusammenhang mit ihren Lehrveranstaltungen unermüdlich darum bemüht, Gesinnungsgenossen zu gewinnen.

The Red Orchestra, however, avoided organizational links with the underground German Communist Party (KPD). Harro Schulze-Boysen and Arvid Harnack envisaged creating a general movement that would transcend party boundaries, and infiltrating Nazi institutions with the long-term goal of setting up a new, classless society, taking up ideas from the prewar youth movement.

Though the group tried, but largely failed, to set up a communications link with the Soviet Union, this was by no means the main thrust of their resistance activities. However, it eventually led to exposure of their contacts and to widespread arrests by the Gestapo. The picture of a Communist espionage organization that emerged in the early years of the Federal German Republic was a reflection of the Cold War, even if members of the group did exchange information with Soviet liaison officers before June 1941.

The exhibition by Franz Rudolf Knubel focuses on the American-born university instructor Mildred Harnack. She represents cosmopolitanism in the resistance group, as well as reflecting the roots of this group—which came mainly from the upper-middle class—in Germany's idealistic educational tradition. At the same time as she was obtaining information on foreign politics through her contacts with the US Embassy, she was supporting underground political activity and working tirelessly to win over people with similar opinions, particularly in the institutions where she taught.

In the exhibition, based partly on the moving biography by Shareen Brysac, Franz Rudolf Knubel presents a carefully drawn picture of Mildred Harnack with her patriotic feeling for Germany. He makes us aware once again of the places where she lived and worked, and reminds us of the humanist legacy that lay in her resistance to the Nazi regime's inhumanity,

In memoriam Mildred Harnack-Fish

Gedenkstätte Deutscher Widerstand
German Resistance Memorial Center

Das von Franz Rudolf Knubel in der Ausstellung behutsam vorgestellte Bild dieser deutschen Patriotin, das sich auf die ergreifende Biografie von Shareen Brysac stützen kann, ruft die Orte ihres Lebensweges wieder ins Bewusstsein und erinnert an das humanistische Vermächtnis, das in ihrem Widerstand gegen Unmenschlichkeit, Rassenhass und Terror des NS-Regimes liegt. Knubels Hommage an Mildred Harnack ist zugleich ein eindrucksvolles Plädoyer dafür, die Tätigkeit der Roten Kapelle von der Kruste des Vorurteils und Missverständnisses zu befreien, die sowohl im Zweiten Weltkrieg als im Kalten Krieg zur Verzerrung ihres Bildes geführt haben. Ihm geht es darum, sie als unverzichtbaren Bestandteil der Geschichte des deutschen Widerstandes gegen Hitler herauszustellen.

Professor Franz Rudolf Knubel verdient dafür unsere Anerkennung, desgleichen die Gedenkstätte Deutscher Widerstand in Berlin und die Sponsoren, welche zur Realisierung der Ausstellung beigetragen haben.

Hans Mommsen
Feldafing, im Frühjahr 2007

racial hatred and terror. But Knubel's homage to Mildred Harnack is also a powerful plea to free the activities of the Red Orchestra from the encrusted prejudice and misunderstanding that resulted in a distorted picture of the group during the Second World War and the Cold War. Knubel is concerned to show the group as an indispensable part of the history of German resistance against Hitler.

Professor Franz Rudolf Knubel deserves our appreciation for this, as do the German Resistance Memorial Center in Berlin and the sponsors who have helped to make this exhibition possible.

Hans Mommsen
Feldafing, spring 2007

Mildred Harnack-Fish in Gremsmühlen am Dieksee,
Juni 1938 (oben) und als Dozentin in Madison, um 1926 (rechts)

Mildred Harnack-Fish at Dieksee, a lake in Gremsmühlen,
June 1938 (above); Mildred Harnack-Fish as a lecturer in Madison,
ca. 1926 (right)

Mildred Harnack-Fish

16. September 1902–16. Februar 1943

Mildred Fish entstammt einer Kaufmannsfamilie und wächst in Milwaukee im US-Staat Wisconsin auf. Sie lehrt an der Universität Wisconsin in Madison Literaturwissenschaft und lernt dort Arvid Harnack kennen, den sie im Sommer 1926 heiratet. 1931 erhält Mildred Harnack eine Anstellung als Lektorin für amerikanische Literaturgeschichte an der Berliner Universität. 1932 wird sie entlassen und beginnt als Lehrerin für englische Literatur und Literaturgeschichte am Berliner Abendgymnasium zu arbeiten. Mit ihren Schülern Karl Behrens, Bodo Schlösinger und Wilhelm Utech setzt eine regelmäßige Schulungstätigkeit zu ökonomischen und politischen Themen unter Leitung ihres Mannes ein. Mildred Harnack nutzt ihre guten Beziehungen zur amerikanischen Botschaft, beschafft Reden von Roosevelt und anderen Politikern, Nachrichten über den Spanischen Bürgerkrieg, Kommentare zu Hitlers Politik und andere Informationen, die sie zusammenstellt und an Gleichgesinnte weitergibt. Sie knüpft Kontakte zu oppositionell oder gegenüber dem NS-Regime kritisch eingestellten Frauen und Männern, gewinnt einige für eine aktive Widerstandstätigkeit und unterstützt die illegale Arbeit von Arvid Harnack. Ende 1941 promoviert sie an der Universität in Gießen und ist Lehrbeauftragte an der Berliner Universität. Sie wird mit ihrem Mann am 7. September 1942 in Preil (Preila) auf der Kurischen Nehrung verhaftet und am 19. Dezember vom Reichskriegsgericht zu sechs Jahren Zuchthaus verurteilt. Am 21. Dezember 1942 hebt Hitler das Urteil auf und beauftragt das Reichskriegsgericht mit einer zweiten Hauptverhandlung, die am 16. Januar 1943 mit der Todesstrafe endet. Mildred Harnack wird am 16. Februar 1943 in Berlin-Plötzensee ermordet.

Mildred Harnack-Fish

September 16, 1902– February 16, 1943

Mildred Fish, whose father was a commercial salesman, grew up in Milwaukee, Wisconsin in the USA. She taught literature at the University of Wisconsin in Madison, where she met Arvid Harnack, whom she married in the summer of 1926. In 1931 Mildred Harnack started working at Berlin University as an instructor for American literary history. She was dismissed in 1932 and started teaching American and English literature and literary history at the Berlin City Night School. She and her pupils Karl Behrens, Bodo Schlösinger and Wilhelm Utech took part in regular study sessions on economic and political topics led by her husband. Mildred Harnack used her good connections to the American embassy and obtained speeches by Roosevelt and other politicians, news about the Spanish Civil War, commentaries on Hitler's politics, and other information that she compiled and passed on to people with similar views. She made contact with men and women who were opposed to or critical of the Nazi regime, persuaded some of them to become active in the resistance, and supported Arvid Harnack's underground activities. She received her doctorate at the university in Gießen at the end of 1941, and taught at Berlin University. On September 7, 1942 she was arrested with her husband in Preil (Preila) on the Curonian Spit. On December 19 she was sentenced to six years' penal servitude by the Reich Court Martial. But on December 21, 1942 Hitler revoked the verdict and ordered the court to conduct a retrial, which ended with the death sentence on January 16, 1943. Mildred Harnack was murdered on February 16, 1943 in Berlin-Plötzensee.

Bei ihrer Verhaftung hat sie einen Band mit Gedichten von Goethe bei sich, von denen sie mehrere noch in der Haft übersetzt. Der Gefängnispfarrer Harald Poelchau rettet diese Übersetzungen, an denen Mildred Harnack noch in den letzten Stunden ihres Lebens arbeitet.

Mildred Harnack-Fish wird von der Berliner Publizistin Margret Boveri einfühlsam charakterisiert: „Sie war für mich mit ihren schönen blonden, straff zurückgekämmten Haaren, ihren klaren, nichts zurückhaltenden Augen der Inbegriff der puritanisch strengen Amerikanerin, die unter der Devise 'high thinking and plain living' lebte. Sie gehörte zu der Generation studierter Frauen, die an den Fortschritt und an die Besserung der Welt glaubten und selbst in geistiger Arbeit an diesem Aufstieg mitarbeiten wollten. Sie war nicht ohne Ehrgeiz, aber er galt nicht der eigenen Person. Zur Zeit, als sie studierte, wurde in Amerika ganz allgemein die Linke als die Trägerin des aufgeklärten Fortschritts angesehen; die Intellektuellen waren ‚rosa', wenn nicht ‚rot', was nicht mit kommunistisch gleichzusetzen war …"

Mildred Harnack took a book of Goethe's poems with her when she was arrested, and translated some of the poems while in prison. The prison chaplain, Harald Poelchau, saved these translations, which Mildred Harnack worked on even during the final hours of her life.

Margret Boveri, a journalist from Berlin, gave a sensitive description of Mildred Harnack-Fish: "With her beautiful blonde hair tightly combed back and her clear eyes that concealed nothing, for me she was the epitome of the strict, puritanical American woman who lived by the motto 'high thinking and plain living'. She belonged to the generation of educated women who believed in progress and a better world, and wanted to contribute to this advance themselves with their intellectual work. She was not without ambition, but not for herself personally. In America at the time when she was a student, the left was quite generally seen as the upholder of enlightened progress; the intellectuals were 'pink', if not 'red', which was not the same as being communist…"

Berlin-Neukölln, Hasenheide 61 „In ihrer Wohnung im vierten Stock dieses Hauses organisierte das Ehepaar Harnack 1933/34 antifaschistische Schulungskurse und politische Gesprächskreise. Dies war der Beginn des vielfältigen Widerstandskampfes der Harnack/Schulze-Boysen-Organisation gegen Nazi-Diktatur und Krieg, für ein humanistisches Deutschland. Über 130 Mitglieder dieser von der Gestapo ‚Rote Kapelle' genannten Gruppe wurden von Sommer 1942 an verhaftet, 49 von ihnen hingerichtet, drei weitere in den Tod getrieben." Text der von dem Bildhauer Volkmar Oellermann gestalteten Gedenktafel für Mildred und Arvid Harnack am Haus Hasenheide 61, Berlin-Neukölln.

The Berlin district of Neukölln, Hasenheide 61 "In 1933/34, Mildred and Arvid Harnack organized anti-fascist study courses and political discussions in their apartment on the fourth floor of this house. This was the beginning of the diverse resistance struggle by the Harnack/Schulze-Boysen organization against the Nazi dictatorship and the war, and for a humanist Germany. The Gestapo called the group the 'Red Orchestra'. From the summer of 1942, over 130 members of the group were arrested. 49 were executed and three others hounded to death." Text of the memorial plaque for Mildred and Arvid Harnack on the house at Hasenheide 61, Berlin-Neukölln, made by the sculptor Volkmar Oellermann.

Franz Rudolf Knubel

Mildred und Arvid Harnack in Potsdam-Neubabelsberg,
Ostern 1940

Mildred and Arvid Harnack in Potsdam-Neubabelsberg,
Easter 1940

Die Rote Kapelle im Widerstand gegen den Nationalsozialismus

Johannes Tuchel

Widerstandsforschung zu betreiben heißt nicht nur, Motive, Ziele und Handlungen von Widerstandskämpferinnen und Widerstandskämpfern in ihrem historischen Kontext zu analysieren. Es bedeutet auch, die Folgen und die Nachwirkungen seit 1945 mit in den Blick zu nehmen. Dabei spielte nicht nur die nationalsozialistische Überlieferung immer wieder eine Rolle, sondern eindeutig auch der deutsch-deutsche Systemkonflikt bis 1989. Die Geschichte des Widerstandes gegen den Nationalsozialismus wurde in Ost und West vielfach zweckgebunden interpretiert und damit politisch instrumentalisiert. Dies galt besonders für die Widerstandsgruppe „Rote Kapelle".

Bereits seit Beginn der nationalsozialistischen Herrschaft, verstärkt seit Mitte der 1930er Jahre, entstanden in Berlin um Arvid Harnack und Harro Schulze-Boysen Gruppen unterschiedlichster sozialer und weltanschaulicher Zusammensetzung, die ab 1940 so eng kooperierten, dass von einem Widerstands-Netzwerk gesprochen werden kann.

Vor dem deutschen Überfall auf die UdSSR im Sommer 1941 gab es eine Reihe von Gesprächen zwischen Schulze-Boysen, Harnack und Vertretern der sowjetischen Botschaft in Berlin. Die dabei ausgesprochenen Warnungen vor den deutschen Angriffsvorbereitungen erreichten auch Stalin, der ihnen aber keinen Glauben schenkte. Die Berliner Gruppe war zudem bereit,

The Red Orchestra in the Resistance against National Socialism

Johannes Tuchel

Researching the resistance against National Socialism means not only analyzing the motivations, goals and actions of resistance fighters in their historical context; it also means reviewing the consequences and effects since 1945. It is not just the Nazi legacy that continues to play a role in this context—what is also decisive is the conflict between the two different political and social systems in East and West Germany during the division up to 1989. The history of the resistance against Nazism was interpreted for particular ends in many ways, which meant it was used for political purposes. This applied especially to the "Red Orchestra" resistance group.

From the very beginning of Nazi rule, and increasingly from the mid-1930s, groups of people with widely varying social backgrounds and political ideologies gathered around Arvid Harnack and Harro Schulze-Boysen in Berlin. From 1940 these groups cooperated so closely that we can call them a resistance network.

Before the German invasion of the USSR in the summer of 1941, there was a series of discussions between Schulze-Boysen, Harnack, and representatives of the Soviet Embassy in Berlin. The warnings they discussed about the German preparations for attack even reached the ears of Stalin, but he did not take them seriously. The Berlin group was also prepared to pass on important military information after the Germans attacked the Soviet Union. However, these

nach dem deutschen Überfall auf die Sowjetunion militärisch wichtige Nachrichten weiterzugeben. Dies scheiterte jedoch an den technischen Unzulänglichkeiten der von der sowjetischen Botschaft zur Verfügung gestellten Funkgeräte. Seit dem Winter 1941/42 kam es dann zu Flugschriftenaktionen gegen die nationalsozialistischen Gewaltverbrechen und den bereits zu dieser Zeit als verloren angesehenen Krieg, aber auch zu Unterstützungsaktionen für Zwangsarbeiter und verfolgte Juden.

Die Berliner Widerstandskreise wurden 1941/42 von der Geheimen Staatspolizei in den Ermittlungskomplex „Rote Kapelle" einbezogen, der sich gegen Gruppen in Belgien und Frankreich richtete, die in engem Kontakt mit oder für den sowjetischen militärischen Nachrichtendienst (GRU) arbeiteten. Im Zuge der Ermittlungen wurde ein einmaliger Kontakt zwischen Brüssel und Berlin aufgedeckt. Es handelte sich dabei um den Besuch des Brüsseler GRU-Agenten „Kent" in Berlin im Oktober 1941. Die NS-Verfolger konnten einen Funkspruch von Moskau nach Brüssel entschlüsseln, der Berliner Adressen enthielt, und davon ausgehend die Berliner Gruppe aufdecken.

Die Gestapo stellte nicht die Widerstandsaktionen, sondern die angebliche Zusammenarbeit mit sowjetischen Nachrichtendiensten in den Vordergrund ihrer Ermittlungen. Wegen dieses von der Gestapo begründeten Bildes waren die Frauen und Männer der Berliner Widerstandsorganisation um Arvid Harnack und Harro Schulze-Boysen seit 1945 unterschiedlichsten Diffamierungen ausgesetzt. In der Bundesrepublik galten sie seit Anfang der 1950er Jahre in der Weiterführung der Gestapo-Argumentation als Angehörige einer „kommunistischen Spionage- und Agentengruppe". Ausgangspunkt dabei waren vor allem die Aussagen ehemaliger Angehöriger der Geheimen Staatspolizei und des Reichskriegsgerichts. Als Ende der 1940er Jahre ein Ermittlungsverfahren gegen den ehemaligen Ankläger in den NS-Prozessen

plans collapsed due to technical difficulties with the radio equipment provided by the Soviet Embassy. From the winter of 1941/42 the group organized leafleting campaigns against the Nazi crimes of violence and against the war, which they already regarded as lost by that time. As well as this, they organized activities in support of forced laborers and persecuted Jews.

In 1941/42 the Berlin resistance circles were included in the complex of Gestapo investigations into the *Rote Kapelle* ("Red Orchestra"), targeted at groups in Belgium and France who maintained close contact or worked for the Soviet military intelligence service (the GRU). During the investigations a one-off contact between Brussels and Berlin was discovered. It concerned a visit to Berlin in October 1941 by the Brussels GRU agent with the cover name "Kent." The Nazi pursuers succeeded in decoding a radio message from Moscow to Brussels containing addresses in Berlin. This led them to the Berlin group.

The Gestapo was primarily concerned not with the group's resistance activities but with its alleged collaboration with Soviet intelligence services. Because of this image established by the Gestapo, the men and women in the Berlin resistance organization around Arvid Harnack and Harro Schulze-Boysen were subjected to all kinds of defamation after 1945. The Gestapo's viewpoint persisted in West Germany, where from the beginning of the 1950s the organization was designated as a "group of Communist spies and secret agents." This was based mainly on the statements of ex-Gestapo members and officials from the Reich Court Martial. At the end of the 1940s, criminal investigations began into the former prosecutors in the Nazi trials of the Red Orchestra, but they led nowhere. The investigating prosecutor in Lüneburg concurred completely with the perspective of the former persecutors. The defamation of the Red Orchestra reached a sorry climax in 1968, when *Der Spiegel* magazine published a series with

In memoriam Mildred Harnack-Fish

gegen die Rote Kapelle eingeleitet wurde, verlief dieses im Sande. Der ermittelnde Lüneburger Staatsanwalt schloss sich voll und ganz der Sicht der ehemaligen Verfolger an. Ein trauriger Höhepunkt der Diffamierung der Roten Kapelle war 1968 erreicht, als DER SPIEGEL eine Serie unter dem Titel „Kennwort Direktor" veröffentlichte, die das von den ehemaligen Verfolgern geprägte Bild des kommunistischen Agentenrings in seltener Eindringlichkeit spiegelte.

Im Osten Deutschlands dagegen wurde die Geschichte der Widerstandsgruppe Rote Kapelle vom Ministerium für Staatssicherheit (MfS) seit Mitte der 1960er Jahre systematisch im Rahmen der nachrichtendienstlichen Arbeit und der Traditionspflege des MfS erforscht und uminterpretiert. Erst in den 1980er Jahren begann sich im Westen Deutschlands das Bild zu wandeln; viele Unterlagen, in denen sich die Widerstandsaktionen der Roten Kapelle erkennen lassen, waren erst in den 1990er Jahren zugänglich. Heute wird die Berliner Gruppe der Roten Kapelle als ein integraler Bestandteil des Widerstandes gegen den Nationalsozialismus betrachtet.

Nach 1990 konnten die bis dahin verschollen geglaubten, tatsächlich aber im Militärhistorischen Archiv in Prag liegenden Akten des Reichskriegsgerichts über die Rote Kapelle und ein Teil der Moskauer Unterlagen, z. B. Verhörprotokolle von Leopold Trepper und Anatoli Gurewitsch, eingesehen werden. 1991 fand Jürgen Danyel in den National Archives in Washington D. C. die Kopie eines neunzigseitigen Gestapo-Berichts mit dem Titel „Bolschewistische Hoch- und Landesverratsorganisation im Reich und in Westeuropa (Rote Kapelle)", der am 2. Februar 1950 die Geheimhaltungsstufe „Secret" erhalten hatte und erst am 18. Februar 1989 freigegeben worden war. Mit Danyels Fund konnte die Diskussion über die Echtheit und den Stellenwert eines der zentralen Dokumente zur Roten Kapelle weitgehend beendet werden. Zum 50. Jahrestag der Verhaftung der Angehörigen der Roten Kapelle im Herbst 1992 wurde mit dem 1942

the title "Code Word: Director." The picture it painted of a Communist espionage ring reflected with exceptional intensity the image created by the former pursuers of the group.

In East Germany, on the other hand, from the mid-1960s the history of the Red Orchestra resistance group was systematically researched and re-interpreted by the Ministry of State Security (MfS, popularly known as "Stasi"). This was done in the context of intelligence work and the MfS' promotion of Communist tradition. The picture first began to change in West Germany in the 1980s; many files containing recognizable information on the Red Orchestra's resistance activities were not accessible until the 1990s. Today the Berlin Red Orchestra group is regarded as an integral part of the resistance against National Socialism.

After 1990, researchers were able to gain access to the Reich Court Martial files on the Red Orchestra—which had been considered lost but were actually in the Military History archive in Prague—and part of the Moscow files, e.g. records of the interrogations of Leopold Trepper and Anatoly Gurevich. In 1991 Jürgen Danyel found a copy of a 90-page Gestapo report with the title, "Bolshevik Organization of Treason and High Treason in the Reich and Western Europe (Red Orchestra)" in the National Archives in Washington D. C. This report, classified "Secret" on February 2, 1950, was not released until February 18, 1989. Danyel's discovery meant that the discussion on the authenticity and status of one of the key documents on the Red Orchestra could largely be resolved. In the fall of 1992, on the 50th anniversary of the arrests of the members of the Red Orchestra, another, even more important record of the group, the album compiled by the Gestapo in 1942 containing the photos of the arrested members, was published in full. This publication by Regina Griebel, Marlies Coburger, and Heinrich Scheel combined and contrasted the Gestapo photos with comprehensive biographies and personal photos as well as facts on the arrests, trials, and executions. The focus shifted from

von der Geheimen Staatspolizei erstellten Fotoalbum mit den Aufnahmen der Festgenommenen ein weiteres, noch wichtigeres Dokument zur Roten Kapelle komplett publiziert. Regina Griebel, Marlies Coburger und Heinrich Scheel stellten dabei Gestapo-Aufnahmen auch ausführliche Biografien und persönliche Fotos sowie Verhaftungs-, Prozess- und Hinrichtungsdaten gegenüber. Nicht die Sichtweise der Verfolger, sondern die Lebenswirklichkeit und die Aktivitäten der Widerstandskämpfer rückten damit in den Mittelpunkt. 1994 resümierte ein von Hans Coppi, Jürgen Danyel und Johannes Tuchel herausgegebener Sammelband den Stand der Forschung. Seither hat eine Reihe vor allem biografischer Arbeiten das Bild der Roten Kapelle weiter präzisieren können.

Im Folgenden sollen nur zwei Punkte hervorgehoben werden: Zuerst gilt es, sich von dem Bild einer einheitlichen, straff geführten und zentralistisch ausgerichteten Widerstandsorganisation zu verabschieden. Die Gruppe unterschied sich nicht nur soziologisch, sondern auch auf der weltanschaulich-ideologischen Ebene grundsätzlich von den kommunistisch geführten Organisationen der Kriegszeit in Berlin, im Ruhrgebiet oder in Hamburg. Die eigentliche Formierungsphase der Roten Kapelle fiel – so der heutige Stand der Überlegungen – in die Zeit nach dem deutschen Überfall auf Polen am 1. September 1939. 1940 begann ein regelmäßiger Meinungsaustausch zwischen den Kreisen um Harnack und Schulze-Boysen. Unklar ist nach wie vor, welche Bedeutung dabei die Diskussion über die deutsch-sowjetischen Nichtangriffsverträge spielte. Sicher ist aber, dass die Vorbereitungen für den deutschen Überfall auf die Sowjetunion das auslösende Moment für die intensivste Phase des Widerstandes waren.

In der Folgezeit sind mehrere Formen und Aktivitäten des Widerstandes der Roten Kapelle zu unterscheiden. Zu ihnen gehörten nach der Sammlung von militärisch wichtigen Nachrichten und dem gescheiterten Versuch ihrer Weitergabe an die Sowjetunion vor allem gezielte Flug-

the standpoint of the pursuers to the actual lives and activities of the resistance members. In 1994 an anthology edited by Hans Coppi, Jürgen Danyel and Johannes Tuchel summarized the state of research. Since then, a series of works, particularly biographies, has contributed to gaining a more detailed picture of the Red Orchestra.

There are two points to be emphasized in the following account. The first concerns getting away from the image of a unified, tightly controlled resistance organization with centralist tendencies. The group was fundamentally different—not just sociologically but also in terms of ideology and worldview—from the Communist-led organizations in Berlin, the Ruhr region, or Hamburg during the war. Current estimations locate the actual formation phase of the Red Orchestra in the period after Germany invaded Poland on September 1, 1939. 1940 saw the start of a regular exchange of opinion between the circles around Harnack and Schulze-Boysen. It is still not clear what role the discussion on the German-Soviet Non-Aggression Pact played in this. What is certain, however, is that Germany's preparations for attacking the Soviet Union gave the impetus for launching the group's most intensive phase of resistance.

Looking at the following period, we should differentiate between several forms of resistance and activities in the Red Orchestra. These included gathering important military information and the unsuccessful attempt to pass it on to the Soviet Union. But above all, there were the targeted leafleting campaigns in the winter of 1941/42, which disseminated information not only about the war—which was already lost—but also about Nazi crimes of violence.

Most of the legends circulated have been about the collaboration between the Red Orchestra and the Soviet Union and the allegedly large number of radio messages from Berlin. For this reason, for our second point it is important to outline briefly the real relationship between

schriftenaktionen im Winter 1941/42, in denen nicht nur über den bereits verlorenen Krieg, sondern auch über die nationalsozialistischen Gewaltverbrechen informiert wurde.

Die meisten Legenden sind über die Zusammenarbeit der Roten Kapelle mit der Sowjetunion und die angebliche Vielzahl der Funksprüche aus Berlin verbreitet worden. Daher sollen im Folgenden als zweiter Punkt – unter Auswertung aller nunmehr vorhandenen Quellen – die tatsächlichen Beziehungen zwischen Berlin und Moskau kurz dargestellt werden: Durch seine Tätigkeit 1930/31 für die „Arbeitsgemeinschaft zum Studium der sowjetischen Planwirtschaft" („Arplan") besaß Arvid Harnack lockere Verbindungen zur sowjetischen Handelsvertretung und Botschaft, besonders zu deren Mitarbeiter Sergej Alexejewitsch Bessonow, der 1938 in die UdSSR zurückgerufen, im Bucharin-Prozess wegen angeblicher Verbindungen zwischen Trotzkisten und Deutschen zu einer 15-jährigen Haftstrafe verurteilt und Ende 1941 erschossen wurde. Harnack vertiefte seine Kontakte zu A. W. Hirschfeld, von 1931 bis 1935 Sekretär in der sowjetischen Botschaft, der auch die „Arplan" unterstützt hatte. Gleichzeitig verstand es Harnack, über seine Frau Mildred gute Beziehungen zur amerikanischen Botschaft in Berlin zu knüpfen, besonders zum amerikanischen Botschafter William Dodd und seiner Tochter Martha. Später waren die Harnacks eng mit Botschaftsrat Donald Heath und dessen Frau Louise befreundet.

1940 lernte Harnack Alexander Michailowitsch Korotkow kennen, der unter dem Namen „Alexander Erdberg" als Botschaftssekretär in Berlin tätig war. Im September 1940 informierte er diesen in einem Gespräch über die Vorbereitungen für den deutschen Überfall auf die Sowjetunion. Ziel des Krieges sei die Abtrennung des westeuropäischen Teiles der Sowjetunion auf der Linie Leningrad—Schwarzes Meer und die Errichtung eines von Deutschland abhängigen Staatengebildes.

Berlin and Moscow, taking into account the evaluation of all the sources now available. Arvid Harnack, through his work for the Working Group for the Study of the Soviet Planned Economy ("Arplan") in 1930/31, had informal contact with the Soviet trade mission and embassy, particularly with an embassy official named Sergei Alexeyevich Bessonov, who was recalled to the Soviet Union in 1938. Bessonov was sentenced to 15 years' imprisonment in the Bukharin Trial because of alleged links between Trotskyists and Germans, and was executed by firing squad at the end of 1941. Harnack had increased contact with A. W. Hirschfeld, a secretary at the Soviet Embassy from 1931 to 1935 who had also supported "Arplan." At the same time Harnack was well able to maintain good relations with the American Embassy in Berlin through his wife Mildred, especially with the American Ambassador, William Dodd, and his daughter, Martha. The Harnacks later became good friends of the Embassy Counselor, Donald Heath, and his wife, Louise.

In 1940 Harnack met Alexander Michailovich Korotkov, who was working as an embassy secretary in Berlin under the name of Alexander Erdberg. At a meeting with Korotkov in September 1940, Harnack told him about Germany's preparations to attack the Soviet Union. He said that the goal of this war was to separate the western European part of the Soviet Union along the Leningrad— Black Sea line, and to establish a German satellite state.

In March 1941 Harnack informed Korotkov about aerial photographs from German long-range espionage aircraft above Soviet territory. Harnack had obtained the information from Schulze-Boysen, who was working at the time in the attaché group on the Air Force General Staff at Wildpark-West. Referring to discussions by officers on the Air Force General Staff, Harnack informed Korotkov that the date of the German operation had been set for the end of April or the beginning of May 1941. He reported on the Air Force General Staff's plans to bomb

Franz Rudolf Knubel

Im März 1941 informierte Harnack Korotkow über Luftaufnahmen der deutschen Fernaufklärung über sowjetischem Territorium. Die Informationen hatte Harnack von Schulze-Boysen erhalten, der zu dieser Zeit in der Attachégruppe im Generalstab der Luftwaffe in Wildpark-West arbeitete. Harnack teilte unter Berufung auf Gespräche von Offizieren im Generalstab der Luftwaffe mit, dass der Termin für die deutsche Operation auf Ende April/Anfang Mai 1941 festgelegt worden sei, berichtete über die Pläne zur Bombardierung von Leningrad, Wyborg, Kiew und Jassa, die im Generalstab der Luftwaffe geplant wurden, gab aber auch eine Einschätzung Schulze-Boysens weiter, der hinter den Angriffsvorbereitungen nur einen „Bluff" vermutete und dem Angriff nur eine Wahrscheinlichkeit von 50 Prozent gab. Ende März 1941 fand ein erstes Treffen zwischen Korotkow, Schulze-Boysen und Harnack in Harnacks Wohnung statt. Weitere Treffen wurden vereinbart, bei denen Schulze-Boysen zusätzliche Informationen aus dem Generalstab der Luftwaffe übermittelte.

Im Mai 1941 berichtete Schulze-Boysen Korotkow über die Möglichkeit eines unmittelbar bevorstehenden Angriffs. Korotkow gab über den sowjetischen Botschafter W. G. Dekanossow diese Mitteilung nach Moskau weiter. Berija und Stalin glaubten der Warnung jedoch nicht. Noch am 21. Juni 1941 schrieb Berija an Stalin: „Ich bestehe erneut auf der Abberufung und Bestrafung unseres Botschafters in Berlin, Dekanossow, der uns wie bisher mit der Mär bombardiert, dass Hitler einen Überfall auf die UdSSR vorbereiten würde. Er berichtet, daß dieser ‚Überfall' morgen stattfindet […] Das gleiche hat Generalmajor W. I. Tupikow, Militärattaché in Berlin, per Funk übermittelt. Dieser dämliche General behauptet unter Berufung auf seine Berliner Agentur, daß drei Wehrmachtsgruppen Moskau, Leningrad und Kiew angreifen werden. Er fordert in frecher Weise, daß wir diese Lügner auch noch mit Funktechnik versorgen sollen. […] Aber ich und meine Leute, Jossif Wissarionowitsch, erinnern uns gut an ihre weise Voraussage: 1941 wird uns Hitler nicht angreifen!"

Leningrad, Vyborg, Kiev, and Yassa, but also passed on Schulze-Boysen's assessment that the preparations for attack were merely "bluff" and there was only a 50 % chance that the attack would actually happen. An initial meeting between Korotkov, Schulze-Boysen and Harnack was held in Harnack's apartment at the end of March 1941. They agreed on further meetings, at which Schulze-Boysen passed on additional information from the Air Force General Staff.

In May 1941 Schulze-Boysen reported to Korotkov on the likelihood of an attack in the immediate future. Korotkov passed on this information to Moscow via the Soviet Ambassador, W. G. Dekanossov. But Beria and Stalin did not believe the warning. As late as June 21, 1941, Beria wrote to Stalin, "I insist again on the recall and punishment of our ambassador in Berlin, Dekanossov, who has been bombarding us like he did previously with the myth that Hitler is preparing to invade the Soviet Union. He reports that this 'ambush' will take place tomorrow… Major General W. I. Tupikov, the military attaché in Berlin, has communicated the same information by radio. The stupid general claims to have information from his Berlin agents' ring that three Wehrmacht groups are to attack Moscow, Leningrad, and Kiev. He even has the cheek to demand that we supply those liars with radio technology… but, Josef Vissarionovich, my staff and I well remember your wise prediction: Hitler will not attack us in 1941!"

To prevent being cut off from the Soviet side in the event of the impending attack, Schulze-Boysen pressed for a direct radio link to Moscow. In mid-June he was given a radio code and 8,000 Reichsmarks. Harnack was more reticent; it took some time and pressure before he also accepted a radio code and 8,000 Reichsmarks from Erdberg in mid-June. Hans Coppi received the first radio set from Erdberg in Kurt and Elisabeth Schumacher's apartment on June 21, 1941. Shortly after, Erdberg handed over a second set to him at Eichkamp S-Bahn

In memoriam Mildred Harnack-Fish

Um bei dem bevorstehenden Angriff nicht von der sowjetischen Seite abgeschnitten zu sein, drängte Schulze-Boysen auf eine direkte Funkverbindung nach Moskau. Er erhielt daraufhin Mitte Juni einen Funkschlüssel und 8 000 Reichsmark. Harnack war zurückhaltender. Erst nach längerem Drängen ließ er sich Mitte Juni von Erdberg einen Funkschlüssel und auch 8 000 Reichsmark übergeben. Das erste Funkgerät erhielt Hans Coppi am 21. Juni 1941 von Erdberg in der Wohnung von Kurt und Elisabeth Schumacher. Kurz darauf übergab Erdberg ihm am S-Bahnhof Eichkamp ein zweites Gerät. Beide Geräte waren nach kurzer Zeit defekt und konnten nicht eingesetzt werden. Lediglich ein Probefunkspruch erreichte Moskau, vermutlich am 21. Juni 1941: „Tausend Grüße allen Freunden!"

Ein drittes, seit 1939 bei Kurt Schulze gelagertes Gerät des militärischen Nachrichtendienstes der UdSSR (GRU) konnte nur für Übungen genutzt werden. Fünf von Harnack verschlüsselte Meldungen, die Coppi über Karl Behrens und Rose Schlösinger erhielt, konnte er deshalb nicht absetzen.

Als sämtliche Nachrichten aus Berlin ausblieben, wandte sich der sowjetische Geheimdienst NKWD Ende August mit der Bitte um Hilfe an den GRU. Leopold Trepper, Pariser Chef des GRU, erhielt die Anweisung, einen Mann nach Berlin zu entsenden. In diesem Funkspruch aus Moskau wurden, wenn auch zum Teil in verstümmelter Form, Namen und Anschriften von Schulze-Boysen, Harnack und Kuckhoff genannt. Ende Oktober 1941 traf Anatoli Gurewitsch („Kent"/ „Sierra") in Berlin ein und setzte sich mit Schulze-Boysen in Verbindung, der ihm von den defekten Funkgeräten berichtete und über die nächsten militärischen Pläne der deutschen Führung informierte. Die in Berlin erhaltenen Meldungen gab Gurewitsch in Brüssel über den dortigen GRU-Funker Johann Wenzel nach Moskau weiter.

station. Before long, both sets were defective and unusable. All that reached Moscow (probably on June 21, 1941) was a test message, "A big hello to all our friends!"

A third radio set from the Soviet military intelligence service (GRU) had been stored in Kurt Schulze's apartment since 1939, but could only be used for practice. Through Karl Behrens and Rose Schlösinger, Coppi received five messages encoded by Harnack, but was unable to transmit them. At the end of August, after failing to receive any messages from Berlin, the Soviet secret service (NKWD) asked the GRU for help. Leopold Trepper, the head of the GRU in Paris, received a radio message from Moscow instructing him to send an agent to Berlin. The message included the names and addresses of Schulze-Boysen, Harnack and Kuckhoff, partly in abbreviated form. At the end of October 1941, Anatoly Gurevich (cover name "Kent" or "Sierra") arrived in Berlin and contacted Schulze-Boysen. The latter told him about the defective radio sets and gave him information about the German leadership's forthcoming military plans. On his return to Brussels, Gurevich passed on the information he had received in Berlin to Moscow via the Brussels GRU radio operator, Johann Wenzel.

In the following period the Berlin group had no success either in making their own radio sets operative, or in passing on further information to Brussels or Moscow via courier or other channels. It was not until August 1942 that they obtained another radio set from the parachutist Albert Hößler, who gave it to Elisabeth Schumacher. But before Hans Coppi could succeed in transmitting, the Berlin group was exposed. The legend of the successful radio operators from the Berlin Red Orchestra is thus reduced to the fact of a single visit from Brussels in October 1941. The group was ready to pass on information, and this was a legitimate intention; but it could not be put into action.

In der Folgezeit gelang es der Berliner Gruppe weder, die eigenen Funkgeräte in Gang zu setzen, noch, weitere Nachrichten nach Brüssel oder Moskau über Kuriere oder andere Kanäle weiterzuleiten. Erst im August 1942 gelangte mit dem Fallschirmspringer Albert Hößler ein weiteres Gerät zu Elisabeth Schumacher. Noch bevor Sendeversuche von Hans Coppi erfolgreich waren, wurde die Berliner Gruppe aufgedeckt. Die Legende von den erfolgreichen Funkern der Berliner Roten Kapelle ist damit auf die Realität eines Besuches aus Brüssel im Oktober 1941 reduziert. Die Bereitschaft zur Weitergabe von Nachrichten war zwar vorhanden und auch legitim; sie konnte aber nicht realisiert werden.

Bereits im Spätsommer 1941 war die Erfolglosigkeit der Funkversuche erkennbar gewesen. Die Diskussion in der Gruppe richtete sich verstärkt darauf, gezielt mit Flugschriften über die NS-Verbrechen im Osten zu informieren und die Kontakte zu anderen Widerstandsgruppen zu intensivieren. Im Kreis um Harro Schulze-Boysen wurde im Winter 1941/42 die Flugschrift „Die Sorge um Deutschlands Zukunft geht durch das Volk" mit Vorstellungen zur Beendigung des Krieges und einer politischen Neuordnung Deutschlands entworfen. Gezielt wurden aus Telefon- und Adressenverzeichnissen Menschen ausgewählt, deren Position ein Interesse für die regimekritischen Informationen der Gruppe erwarten ließ. John Graudenz, Helmut Himpel, Maria Terwiel und andere übernahmen die Herstellung und den Versand in mehreren hundert Exemplaren. Im Februar 1942 erfasste die Gestapo über 260 Flugschriften, einen Monat später wurden die Ermittlungen jedoch als „aussichtslos" eingestellt.

Der Winter 1941/42 stand auch sonst im Zeichen vielfältiger Aktivitäten des Widerstandes. Einige Mitglieder der Gruppe sammelten Informationen, andere schrieben Flugblätter, vervielfältigten und verteilten sie oder stellten Verbindungen zu Widerstandsgruppen her, die sich in Berlin, Hamburg, Mitteldeutschland oder in Bayern gebildet hatten. Im Mittelpunkt standen

By the late summer of 1941, the group already acknowledged that its attempts at radio transmission were futile. Discussions within the group increasingly turned to disseminating leaflets with information on the Nazi crimes in Eastern Europe, and building closer contact with other resistance groups. In the winter of 1941/42, members of the circle around Harro Schulze-Boysen wrote a leaflet, "The People are Troubled about Germany's Future." It included ideas about ending the war and creating a new political order in Germany. Using telephone directories and address lists, the group deliberately selected the names of people whose position indicated that they might have an interest in critical information about the regime. John Graudenz, Helmut Himpel, Maria Terwiel, and other group members were responsible for producing and dispatching several hundred copies of the leaflet. In February 1942 the Gestapo registered over 260 leaflets, but a month later the investigations were dropped as "futile."

The resistance was also active in many other ways during the winter of 1941/42. Some members of the group gathered information, others wrote, duplicated, and distributed leaflets, or made contact with resistance groups that had been formed in Berlin, Hamburg, central Germany, and Bavaria. The focus was now on attempts to inform the public about the Nazi crimes of violence and to encourage active or passive resistance. The pamphlets, titled "Open Letters to the Eastern Front," gave detailed descriptions of the Nazi crimes of violence. The idea of being on an "inner front" gave the name to an underground publication that appeared several times. Its articles were addressed not only to Germans but also to forced laborers from other countries and prisoners of war. The articles openly called for action against the Nazi dictatorship and reminded people of their individual political responsibility. The group's activities became more open, but this gave rise to some internal controversy because of the risks involved. On the night of May 17/18, 1942, flyposted leaflets appeared in several districts of Berlin protesting against the Nazi propaganda exhibition, *The Soviet Paradise*. They were

In memoriam Mildred Harnack-Fish

Gedenkstätte Deutscher Widerstand
German Resistance Memorial Center

jetzt Versuche, die Öffentlichkeit über die nationalsozialistischen Gewaltverbrechen zu informieren und zu aktivem und passivem Widerstand aufzufordern. Die „Offnen Briefe an die Ostfront" schilderten ausführlich die NS-Gewaltverbrechen. Die Vorstellung, an einer „inneren Front" zu stehen, gab einer mehrfach erscheinenden Untergrundschrift ihren Namen. Ihre Texte wandten sich nicht nur an Deutsche, sondern auch an ausländische Zwangsarbeiter und Kriegsgefangene. Sie riefen offen zu Aktionen gegen die NS-Diktatur auf und wiesen jeden Einzelnen auf seine politische Verantwortung hin. Die Aktionen wurden offener, waren aber wegen des damit verbundenen Risikos in der Gruppe nicht unumstritten. In der Nacht vom 17. auf den 18. Mai 1942 tauchten in mehreren Berliner Stadtbezirken Klebezettel auf, die gegen die große nationalsozialistische Propaganda-Ausstellung *Das Sowjetparadies* protestieren sollten. Sie waren von Männern und Frauen der Gruppe, als Liebespaare getarnt, geklebt worden und verursachten großes Aufsehen.

Im August 1942 entschlüsselte die Dechiffrierabteilung beim Oberkommando des Heeres den Funkspruch aus Moskau an den Agenten „Kent" in Brüssel mit den Adressen von Kuckhoff und Schulze-Boysen. Die Gestapo verhaftete am 31. August zuerst Harro Schulze-Boysen und bis März 1943 mehr als 120 Männer und Frauen. Am 19. Dezember 1942 verurteilte das Reichskriegsgericht in einem ersten Prozess zehn Angeklagte zum Tode. Hitler bestätigte am 21. Dezember 1942 die Todesurteile und befahl für Harro Schulze-Boysen, Arvid Harnack, Kurt Schumacher und John Graudenz die sofortige Vollstreckung durch den Strang. Für die zu Zuchthausstrafen verurteilten Erika von Brockdorff und Mildred Harnack ordnete er die Neuverhandlung an. Mitte Januar 1943 wurden auch sie zum Tode verurteilt. Weitere 19 Prozesse mit zahlreichen Todesurteilen folgten. Insgesamt wurden mehr als fünfzig Mitglieder dieser Gruppe ermordet.

pasted up by men and women from the group disguised as courting couples, and attracted considerable attention.

In August 1942 the cryptography department of the Army High Command decoded the radio message from Moscow to "Kent," the agent in Brussels, with the addresses of Kuckhoff and Schulze-Boysen. On August 31 the Gestapo first of all arrested Harro Schulze-Boysen; by March 1943 over 120 men and women had been taken into custody. In the first trial on December 19, 1942, the Reich Court Martial sentenced ten defendants to death. Hitler endorsed the death sentences on December 21, 1942 and ordered that Harro Schulze-Boysen, Arvid Harnack, Kurt Schumacher, and John Graudenz be executed immediately by hanging. He ordered retrials for Erika von Brockdorff and Mildred Harnack, who had been sentenced to penal servitude. In mid-January 1943 they were also sentenced to death. There were 19 subsequent trials with a large number of death sentences. In all, over 50 members of the group were legally murdered.

If we try to sum up the Red Orchestra's varied resistance activities on the basis of the new state of research, we get a picture of a broad range of activities, from practical help and support for victims of persecution to wide distribution of pamphlets and leaflets. After failing in its attempts to transmit messages to the Soviet Union, the group stepped up its activities in giving information to the public. They organized this so well that the Gestapo was unable to track down any clues. There are indications of a process of discussion in the group during the summer of 1942 aimed at stepping up its activities; but these plans had not yet been finalized when the Gestapo pounced in August 1942.

The group's internal discussions on the question of possible developments in Germany after the war had also not been resolved by that time. What is certain is that their ideas were not congruent with those of the German Communist Party leadership in Moscow. The available documents show clearly that the group was not aiming for a Communist system on the

Franz Rudolf Knubel

Versucht man ein Fazit der verschiedenen Widerstandsaktionen der Roten Kapelle vor dem Hintergrund dieses neuen Forschungsstandes, so werden breitgefächerte Aktivitäten sichtbar, die von konkreten Unterstützungshandlungen für Verfolgte bis zur umfangreichen Verbreitung von Flugschriften reichten. Nach dem Scheitern der Nachrichtenübermittlung an die Sowjetunion verstärkte die Gruppe ihre Bemühungen zur Aufklärung der Öffentlichkeit. Sie organisierte dies so gut, dass die Gestapo keinerlei Hinweise ermitteln konnte. Im Sommer 1942 war ein Diskussionsprozess erkennbar, der zur Verstärkung der Aktivitäten führen sollte. Diese Planungen waren noch nicht abgeschlossen, als im August 1942 die Gestapo zugriff. Auch die gruppeninternen Erörterungen zu den Fragen einer möglichen Nachkriegsentwicklung in Deutschland waren zu dieser Zeit noch nicht beendet. Sicher ist, dass diese sich nicht mit den Vorstellungen der Moskauer KPD-Führung deckten. Die vorliegenden Dokumente zeigen jedoch eindeutig, dass ein kommunistisches System stalinistischer Prägung nicht die Zielvorstellung war. Eine sorgfältige Analyse der vorhandenen Flugschriften wird zeigen müssen, ob genauere Aussagen über jene sozialistische Demokratie möglich sind, die diese Gruppe wollte. Offen bleibt, wie weit sie sich Gesellschafts- und Denkmodellen hätten nähern können, wie sie in den folgenden Jahren etwa von der Weißen Rose oder dem Kreisauer Kreis entwickelt wurden.

Sicher ist, dass die Mitglieder dieser Gruppe weltanschaulich und soziologisch unterschiedlichsten Traditionen angehörten und dass sie sich nicht mehr in den alten Traditionen der Weimarer Politik sahen. Auch auf die besondere Bedeutung der Frauen in dieser Gruppe sei an dieser Stelle noch einmal hingewiesen. Offen sind weiterhin Fragen nach den Biografien der Beteiligten und der Entwicklung der einzelnen Kreise in den Jahren 1935 bis 1939 sowie nach dem Verhalten der sowjetischen Stellen und dem Kalkül dahinter. Beendet ist auch noch nicht die Diskussion über die Diffamierung und Verzeichnung der Roten Kapelle in West und Ost nach 1945.

Stalinist model. It would require careful examination of the surviving leaflets and pamphlets to see whether it is possible to make more precise statements about the kind of socialist democracy this group wanted. It remains an open question as to how close they could have come to the social and philosophical models developed in the following years by groups like the White Rose and the Kreisau Circle.

What is certain is that the members of this group belonged to a very wide variety of ideological and sociological traditions and no longer saw themselves as part of the old tradition of Weimar politics. At this point it is worth reiterating the particular importance of women in the group. There are still open questions about the personal life stories of the people involved and the development of the individual circles from 1935 to 1939, as well as the attitude of the Soviet authorities and the calculation that lay behind it. And the debate about the defamation and distorted portrayal of the Red Orchestra in West and East Germany after 1945 has yet to be concluded.

Mildred Harnack-Fish

16. September 1902 Milwaukee, Wisconsin–16. Februar 1943 Berlin-Plötzensee, hier mit ihrem Ehemann Arvid Harnack bei Saalfeld, 1930, der als Mitglied der „Roten Kapelle" bereits am 22. Dezember 1942 hingerichtet wurde.

Mildred Harnack-Fish

September 16, 1902 Milwaukee, Wisconsin–February 16, 1943 Berlin-Plötzensee, with her husband Arvid Harnack near Saalfeld, 1930. Arvid Harnack was executed as a member of the "Red Orchestra" on December 22, 1942.

Franz Rudolf Knubel

Mildred Harnack-Fish übersetzte handschriftlich in einem Exemplar des 1941 im
Potsdamer Verlag Rütten & Loening erschienenen Gedichtbandes *Das Göttliche*
von Johann Wolfgang von Goethe.

> Mildred Harnack-Fish wrote her own translations of some of the poems in her
> copy of the poetry book *Das Göttliche* ("The Divine") by Johann Wolfgang von
> Goethe, published in 1941 by Rütten & Loening Verlag, Potsdam.

In memoriam Mildred Harnack-Fish

Gedenkstätte Deutscher Widerstand
German Resistance Memorial Center

Noch am 16. Februar 1943, am Tag ihrer Hinrichtung in Berlin-Plötzensee, hat die amerikanische Literaturwissenschaftlerin Mildred Harnack-Fish an der Übersetzung des Goethe-Gedichtes „Vermächtnis" gearbeitet: „Kein Wesen kann zu nichts zerfallen! / Das Ew'ge regt sich fort in allen, / Am Sein ..." Sprache bewegte sie bis in den Tod. Schreiben bannte das Grauen. Ihre letzten Worte waren: „... und ich habe Deutschland so geliebt."

On February 16, 1943, the day of her execution in Berlin-Plötzensee, the American literary scholar Mildred Harnack-Fish continued working on her translation of Goethe's poem "Vermächtnis" ("Legacy"): "No being can to nothing fall. / The Everlasting lives in all. / Sustain yourself in joy…" Language moved her up to the moment of her death. Writing held the horror at bay. Her last words were, "…and I have loved Germany so much."

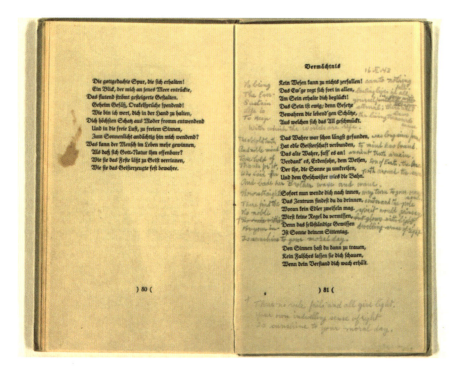

16. II. 43
No being can to nothing fall.
The Everlasting lives in all.
Sustain yourself in joy with life.
Life is eternal; there are laws
To keep the living treasure's cause
With which the worlds are rife.

The old old truth was long since found
And noble mind to mind has bound.
Take hold of ancient truth amain.
Thank for it, son of Earth, the One
Who laid her path around the sun
And bade her Brother wax and wane.

Now straight way turn to your own soul.
There find the center and the pole
No noble spirit would gainsay.
There no rule fails and all give light.
Your own indwelling sense of right
Is sunshine to your moral day.

... zur kleinsten Schar / ...with a chosen few

In memoriam Mildred Harnack-Fish

Gedenkstätte Deutscher Widerstand
German Resistance Memorial Center

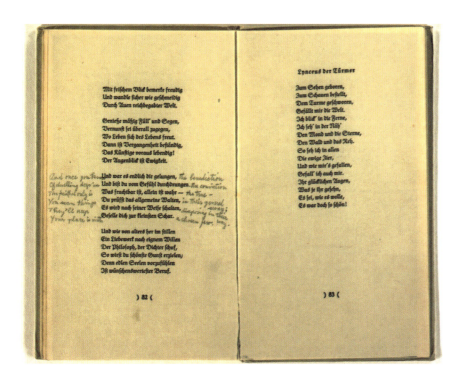

And once you know the benediction
Of dwelling deep in the conviction
The fruitful only is the true —
You scan things in their general sway;
They'll keep disposing in their way.
Your place is with a chosen few.

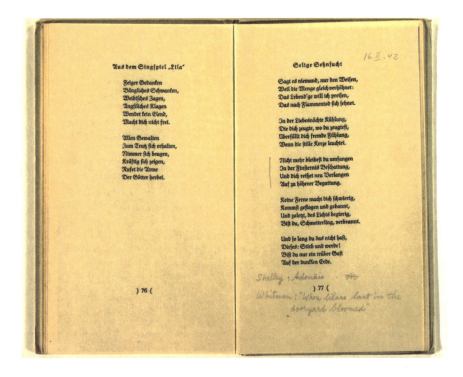

16. II. 42

Shelley: Adonäis

Whitman: "When lilacs last in the dooryard bloomed"

In memoriam Mildred Harnack-Fish

... zur kleinsten Schar /...with a chosen few

Gedenkstätte Deutscher Widerstand
German Resistance Memorial Center

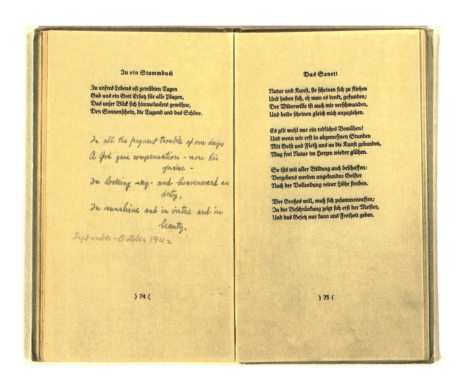

In all the frequent trouble of our days
A God gave compensation — more his praise —
In looking sky- and heavenward as duty,
In sunshine and in virtue and in beauty.

September–October 1942

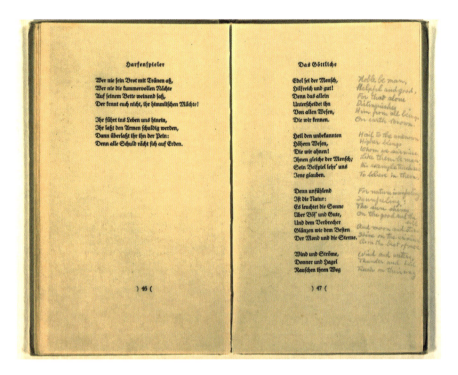

Noble be man,
Helpful and good,
For that alone
Distinguishes
Him from all beings
On earth known.

Hail to the unknown
Higher beings
Whom we surmise.
Like them be man;
His example teach us
To believe in them.

For nature is unfeeling
So unfeeling:
The sun shines
On the good and the evil
And moon and stars
Shine on the criminal
And the best of men.

Wind and waters
Thunder and hail
Rush on their way

In memoriam Mildred Harnack-Fish

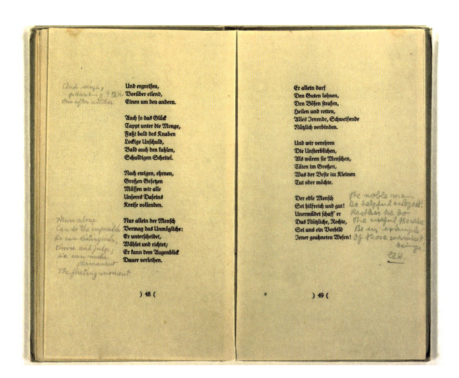

And seize,
Passing   ? A. H.
One after another.

The noble man
Be helpful and good!
Restless he do
The useful, the wise,
Be us example
Of those surmised beings!

             Cl. H.

Man alone
Can do the impossible.
He can distinguish,
Choose and judge;
He can make permanent
The fleeting moment.

Franz Rudolf Knubel

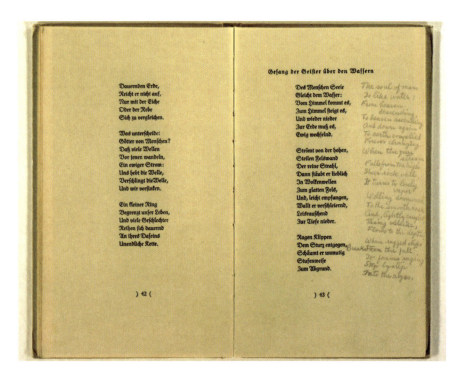

The soul of man
Is like water:
From heaven descending,
To heaven ascending
And down again
To earth compelled
Forever changing.

When the pure stream
Falls from the high
Sheer rock wall,
It turns to lovely vapor
Welling downward
To the smooth rock
And, lightly caught,
Rising veillike,
Flows to the depths.

When rugged cliffs
Break the fall
It foams raging
Step by step
Into the abyss.

In memoriam Mildred Harnack-Fish

... zur kleinsten Schar / ...with a chosen few

Gedenkstätte Deutscher Widerstand
German Resistance Memorial Center

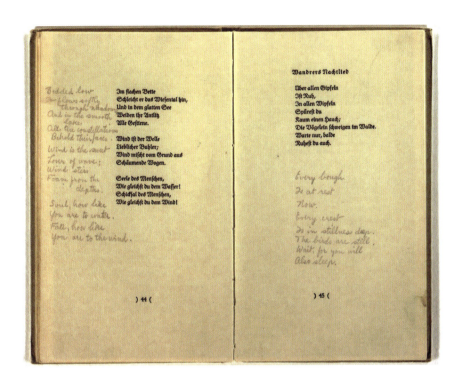

Bedded low
It flows softly through meadows,
And in the smooth lake
All the constellations
Behold their faces.

Wind is the sweet
Lover of wave;
Wind stirs
Foam from the depths.

Soul, how like
You are to water.
Fate, how like
You are to the wind.

Every bough
Is at rest
Now.
Every crest
Is in stillness deep.
The birds are still.
Wait, for you will
Also sleep.

Franz Rudolf Knubel

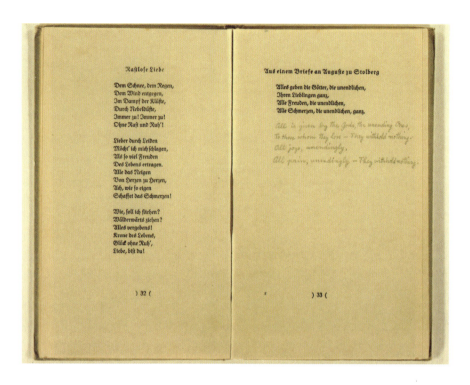

All is given by the Gods, the unending Ones,
To those whom they love — They withhold nothing.
All joys, unendingly,
All pain, unendingly — They withhold nothing.

In memoriam Mildred Harnack-Fish

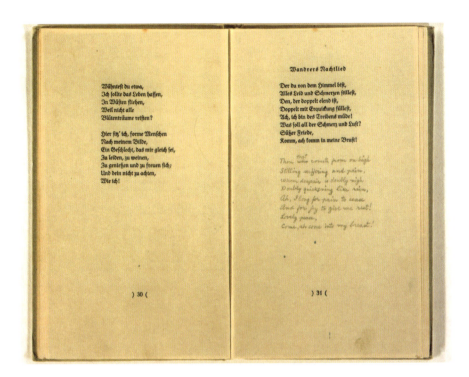

Thou that cometh from on high
Stilling suffering and pain,
Whom despair is doubly nigh
Doubly quickening like rain,
Ah, I long for pain to cease
And for joy to give me rest!
Lovely peace,
Come, ah come into my breast!

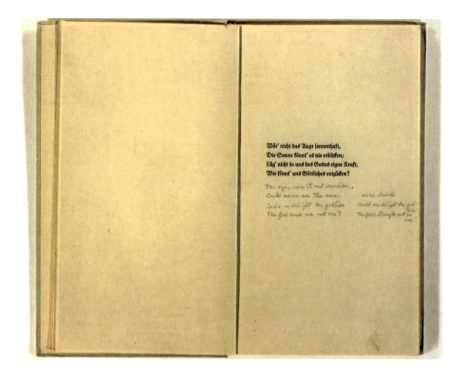

The eye, were it not sunlike,
Could never see the sun.　　　ne'er behold
Could us delight the godlike　Could one delight the godlike
The God and we not one?　　　The God's strength not in one?

In memoriam Mildred Harnack-Fish

... zur kleinsten Schar / ...with a chosen few

Gedenkstätte Deutscher Widerstand
German Resistance Memorial Center

Wandrers Nachtlied

Über allen Gipfeln
Ist Ruh,
In allen Wipfeln
Spürest du
Kaum einen Hauch;
Die Vöglein schweigen im Walde.
Warte nur, balde
Ruhest du auch.

Ich versuche, die historische Person als einen wirklichen Menschen zu fassen, sie gedanklich einzukreisen. Ich lese historische Fakten, die sich über Worte vermitteln, und schreibe. Immer wieder die gleichen Texte. Schreiben als Erinnerungsarbeit: Gedichte von Johann Wolfgang von Goethe und die Übersetzungen von Mildred Harnack-Fish als Befreiung aus der beklemmenden Situation in der Zelle in Plötzensee.

I am trying to grasp the historical personage as a real person, to encompass her with my thoughts. I read historical facts communicated with words, and I write. Always the same texts. Writing as a work of remembrance: poems by Johann Wolfgang von Goethe and the translations by Mildred Harnack-Fish as liberation from the trapped situation in the cell in Plötzensee.

Franz Rudolf Knubel
Exerzitien zu Mildred Harnack-Fish, 2006
Tinte auf Vorsatzpapier
je 98 x 68 cm

Franz Rudolf Knubel
Spiritual Exercises on the theme of Mildred Harnack-Fish, 2006
Ink on endpaper
98 x 68 cm each

Vermächtnis

16.II.43

Kein Wesen kann zu nichts zerfallen!
Das Ew'ge regt sich fort in allen,
Am Sein erhalte dich beglückt!
Das Sein ist ewig; denn Gesetze
Bewahren die lebend'gen Schätze,
Aus welchen sich das All geschmückt.

Das Wahre war schon längst gefunden,
Hat edle Geisterschaft verbunden,
Das alte Wahre fass' es an!
Verdank es, Erdensohn dem Weisen,
Der ihr die Sonne zu umkreisen
Und dem Geschwister wies die Bahn.

Sofort nun wende dich nach innen
Das Zentrum findest du da drinnen,
Woran kein Edler zweifeln mag.
Wirst keine Regel da vermissen,
Denn das selbständige Gewissen
Ist Sonne deinem Sittentag.

Den Sinnen hast du dann zu trauen
Kein Falsches lassen sie dich schauen
Wenn dein Verstand dich wach erhält
Mit frischem Blick bemerke freudig
Und wandle sicher wie geschmeidig
Durch Auen reichbegabter Welt.

Geniesse mässig Füll und Segen,
Vernunft sei überall zugegen,
Wo Leben sich des Lebens freut.
Dann ist Vergangenheit beständig,
Das Künftige voraus lebendig,
Der Augenblick ist Ewigkeit.

Und war es endlich dir gelungen,
Und bist du vom Gefühl durchdrungen,
Was fruchtbar ist allein ist wahr —
Du prüfst das allgemeine Walten,
Es wird nach seiner Weise schalten,
Geselle dich zur kleinsten Schar.

Und wenn von alters her im stillen
Ein Liebeswerk nach eignem Willen
Der Philosoph, der Dichter schuf,
So wirst du schöne Gunst erzielen;
Denn edlen Seelen vorzufühlen
Ist wünschenswertester Beruf.

No being can to nothing fall
The everlasting lives in all
Sustain yourself in joy with life
Life is eternal, there are laws
To keep the living treasure's cause
With which the worlds are rife.

The old old truth was long since found
And noble mind to mind has bound
The hold of ancient truth amain.
Think of it son of Earth the one
Who laid the path around the sun
And bade her Brother waste and crane.

Then straight way turn to your own soul
There find the counterant the pole
No noble spirit would agony.
There no rule fails and all give light.
Your own indwelling sence of right
No sunshine your moral day.

And once you know the benediction
Of dwelling deep in the conviction
The fruitful only is the true —
You scan things in their general sway;
They'll keep dispensing in their way
Your place is with a chosen few.

Gesang der Geister über den Wassern

Des Menschen Seele
Gleicht dem Wasser:
Vom Himmel kommt es,
Zum Himmel steigt es,
Und wieder nieder
Zur Erde muß es,
Ewig wechselnd.

Strömt von der hohen,
Steilen Felswand
Der reine Strahl,
Dann stäubt es lieblich
In Wolkenwellen
Zum glatten Fels,
Und leicht empfangen,
Wallt es verschleiernd,
Leis rauschend
Zur Tiefe nieder.

Ragen Klippen
Dem Sturz entgegen,
Schäumt er unmutig
Stufenweise
Zum Abgrund
Im flachen Bette
Schleicht es das Wiesental hin
Und in dem glatten See
Weiden ihr Antlitz
Alle Gestirne.

Wind in der Welle
Lieblicher Buhler
Wind mischt vom Grund aus
Schäumende Wogen

Seele des Menschen
Wie gleichst du dem Wasser!
Schicksal des Menschen
Wie gleichst du dem Wind!

The soul of man
Is like water
From heaven descending
To heaven ascending
And down again
To earth impelled
Forever changing.

When the pure stream
Falls from the high
Sheer roll wall
It turns to lovely vapor
Welling downward
To the smooth rock
And, lightly caught,
Rising in lice,
Flows to the depth.

When rugged cliffs
Break the fall
It foams raging
Step by step
Into the abyss
Bedded low
It flows softly through meadows
And in the smooth lakes
All the constellations
Behold their faces.

Wind in the sweet
Lover of wave;
Wind stirs
Foam from the depth.

Soul how like
You are to water.
Fate, how like
You are to the wind.

Franz Rudolf Knubel

Orte, auf die Mildred Harnack-Fish ihren Fuß gesetzt hat, wiedererwecken – ein nicht gelingendes Unterfangen, weil die gefundenen Orte Orte des Nicht-Gedenkens sind. Es gibt keine greifbaren Spuren von ihr. Ich zeige Bilder und Faksimiles, um einer Person Gerechtigkeit widerfahren zu lassen, sie dem Vergessen zu entreißen. Der Unterschied zwischen einer Abreibung und einem Foto ist wie der zwischen einer Totenmaske und einer Abbildung der Toten. Aber alles sind nur grobe Näherungen. Es ist nicht ihre Brille, es sind nicht ihre Briefe, ihre Pantoffeln oder ihre Schlafröcke. Trotzdem ist es für mich ein nützlicher Mitleidensgang, *compassion*. Das Knien beim Abreiben empfinde ich als Geste tätiger Verehrung. Ich versuche, eine körperliche Erfahrung zu erleben, ähnlich den Exerzitien der Gläubigen.

Reviving places where Mildred Harnack set foot — an attempt that fails because the places are scenes of non-remembrance. There are no tangible traces of her. I am showing pictures and facsimiles to enable justice to be done to a person, to rescue her from oblivion. The difference between a rubbing and a photo is like that between a death mask and a picture of the dead person. But these are all only rough approaches. It is not her glasses, it is not her letters, her slippers, or her nightgowns. All the same, it is a useful way toward compassion. Kneeling down to make rubbings feels like a gesture of worship. I am trying to have a bodily experience similar to the spiritual exercises of believers.

In memoriam Mildred Harnack-Fish

... zur kleinsten Schar / ...with a chosen few

Gedenkstätte Deutscher Widerstand
German Resistance Memorial Center

Am Fuchspaß 33, Berlin-Zehlendorf, 1. Januar–15. Juli 1932

Am Fuchspaß 33, Berlin-Zehlendorf, January 1–July 15, 1932

Hasenheide 61, Berlin-Neukölln (damals SW29)

Hasenheide 61, Berlin-Neukölln (SW29 at that time)

Tristanstraße 27, Berlin-Nikolassee

Genthiner Straße 46, Berlin-Schöneberg (damals Woyrschstraße 46, W 35, heute Möbel Krieger)

Genthiner Straße 46, Berlin-Schöneberg (then Woyrschstraße 46, W 35, today a furniture store, Möbel Krieger)

In memoriam Mildred Harnack-Fish

... zur kleinsten Schar / ...with a chosen few

Gedenkstätte Deutscher Widerstand
German Resistance Memorial Center

Genthiner Straße 14, Berlin-Schöneberg (damals Woyrschstraße 16, W 35)

Genthiner Straße 14, Berlin-Schöneberg (Woyrschstraße 16, W 35 at that time)

S. Fischer Verlag, Lützowstraße 89–90, Berlin-Tiergarten (damals W 35)

S. Fischer Verlag (publishing house), **Lützowstraße 89–90, Berlin-Tiergarten** (W 35 at that time)

In memoriam Mildred Harnack-Fish

Gedenkstätte Deutscher Widerstand
German Resistance Memorial Center

Humboldt Universität (damals Friedrich-Wilhelms-Universität zu Berlin, C 2)
Spandauer Straße 1, Berlin-Mitte

Humboldt University (Friedrich Wilhelm University Berlin, C 2 at that time)
Spandauer Straße 1, Berlin-Mitte

Städtisches Berliner Abendgymnasium, Wormser Straße 11, Berlin-Schöneberg (damals W 62)

Berlin City Night School, Wormser Straße 11, Berlin-Schöneberg (W 62 at that time)

In memoriam Mildred Harnack-Fish

24. April 2006 18:00 Abfahrt mit der *Lisco Gloria*, einem Container-Frachter mit Passagierteil und Autodeck, von Kiel nach Klaipeda, zusammen mit Eberhard Wolff. Alles gepflegt, rostfrei und nahezu klinisch weiß/blau. Es ist wie eine Wallfahrt, eine Pilgerfahrt, das eigene Fleisch an einen bestimmten Ort zu bringen. Ich musste alle Orte besuchen, die ich erreichen konnte, um Mildred Harnack-Fish näher zu kommen, obwohl ich wusste, dass es aussichtslos ist.

April 24, 2006, 6 p.m. Departure with Eberhard Wolff on the Lisco Gloria, a container freight ship with a passenger section and car deck sailing from Kiel to Klaipeda. It's all well-kept, rust-free and almost clinical in blue-and-white. Going in person to a specific place is like embarking on a pilgrimage. To get closer to Mildred Harnack-Fish, I had to visit all the places I could get to, although I knew it was futile.

26. April 2006 – zwei Tage nach meinem Geburtstag: 68. Sonnenuntergang vor Preila auf der Kurischen Nehrung – ich lebe. Arvid Harnack und Mildred Harnack-Fish wurden in dem Haus in Preil (Preila) am 7. September 1942 von der Gestapo in der Maske der Fremdenpolizei verhaftet.

April 26, 2006 — two days after my birthday: 68. Sunset outside Preila on the Curonian Spit — I am alive. Arvid and Mildred Harnack were arrested on September 7, 1942 in the house in Preil (Preila) by the Gestapo posing as Aliens Police.

16. Februar 2006 Gedenkstätte Plötzensee, Eingang zum ehemaligen Hinrichtungsraum

February 16, 2006 Plötzensee Memorial Center, entrance to the former execution room

Feld 015 Nr. 505 Friedhof Zehlendorf, Onkel-Tom-Straße 30.
In memoriam.

Area 015 No. 505 Zehlendorf Cemetery, Onkel-Tom-Straße 30.
In memoriam.

In memoriam Mildred Harnack-Fish

Gedenkstätte Deutscher Widerstand
German Resistance Memorial Center

„In memoriam" Franz Rudolf Knubel bei der Herstellung einer Abreibung des Grabsteins von Mildred und Arvid Harnack auf dem Friedhof Onkel-Tom-Straße in Berlin-Zehlendorf

"In memoriam" Franz Rudolf Knubel making a rubbing of the gravestone of Mildred and Arvid Harnack in the cemetery in Onkel-Tom-Straße in the Berlin district of Zehlendorf

Franz Rudolf Knubel

„… und ich habe Deutschland so geliebt."
Mildred Harnack-Fish vor ihrer Hinrichtung
am 16. Februar 1943, 18:57 Uhr

"…and I have loved Germany so much."
Mildred Harnack-Fish before her execution
at 6.57 p.m. on February 16, 1943

Franz Rudolf Knubel
Berlin-Plötzensee, Hüttigpfad: Hinrichtungsstätte
1/7–7/7, 2007
Frottagen, Graphit auf Vorsatzpapier
je 100 x 70 cm

Franz Rudolf Knubel
Berlin-Plötzensee, Hüttigpfad: Place of execution 1/7–7/7, 2007
Rubbings, graphite on endpaper
100 x 70 cm each

In memoriam Mildred Harnack-Fish

Gedenkstätte Deutscher Widerstand
German Resistance Memorial Center

10. September 2005 Berlin-Plötzensee Eine rote Kordel teilt den Raum. Über den Fenstern die Stange mit den sechs Haken. Darunter ein Kranz und auf den Fensterbänken vertrocknete Blumen. Ich steige über die Absperrung und packe meine 70 x 100 Bögen Vorsatzpapier und das Kästchen mit den Graphitstiften aus. Die Arbeitshaltung ist Kniefall. Ich bin ruhig und tue, was ich mir als Erinnerungsarbeit vorgenommen habe: Spuren abreiben vom groben Estrich, der zahllose Narben hat. Im vorderen Drittel der abgeteilten Fläche ist ein schmaler Gulli mit sieben eisernen Stegen, nicht viel größer als ein Blatt A4. Dort in unmittelbarer Nähe stand die Maschine zum Töten: das Fallbeil. Erstaunlich ruhig geht alles vor sich, ich beobachte mich, höre mir zu, während ich die Spuren des Eisenrostes auf das Papier übertrage, prüfe das Ergebnis, wiederhole es gleich nochmal auf einem kleineren Bogen Büttenpapier – der zweite Versuch erübrigt sich, ich sehe es gleich.

Es ist still an diesem Morgen, ich spüre nur den Widerstand des Materials und meinen Atem, höre den Graphit auf dem Papier beim Gang durch die Hölle. In den Büchern steht, dass an diesem Ort, so oder so, etwa dreitausend Menschen „Im Namen des Volkes" ermordet wurden. Nach einer halben Stunde bin ich durch, wie man sagt, und ich habe sieben Bögen bis zum Rand voller Spuren. Einmal habe ich das Material gewechselt – unnötig. Die Arbeiten sind ohnehin nur lesbar, wenn sie benannt werden: Exerzitien im Unfassbaren.

Ich bin seltsam leer und suche nach dem nötigen Halt. – Ein eigenartiger Schwebezustand hat sich eingestellt. – Gestern las ich *Paradies verloren* von Cees Noteboom: Über ein Spiel mit Engeln.

September 10, 2005 Berlin-Plötzensee A red cord barrier divides the room. Above the windows, the pole with the six hooks. Below this a wreath, and dried-out flowers on the window ledges. I climb over the barrier and unpack my 70 x 100 cm sheets of tracing paper and the box with the graphite sticks. I am working on my knees. I am calm and doing what I planned as a work of remembrance: making rubbings of traces from the rough floor plaster with its countless scars. In the front part of the divided space is a small gully with seven iron bars, no bigger than a sheet of A 4 paper. Right next to that was the machine for killing: the guillotine. Everything goes remarkably peacefully, I watch myself and listen to myself while I transfer the traces of the iron grating onto the paper, inspect the result, then repeat it again right away on a smaller sheet of handmade paper—I can see immediately that the second attempt is superfluous.

It is quiet this morning; all I can feel is the resistance of the material and my breath, all I can hear is the graphite on the paper on the path through hell. In the books it says that at this spot around three thousand persons were murdered in one way or another, "In the name of the people." After half-an-hour I am through, as they say, and I have seven sheets filled to the edges with traces. At one point I changed the material—not necessary. Anyway, the works are only legible if they are captioned: Spiritual Exercises in the Unimaginable.

I am strangely empty and looking for the support I need.— A strange floating state has set in.— Yesterday I read *Paradise Lost* by Cees Noteboom: about a game with angels.

In memoriam Mildred Harnack-Fish

Gedenkstätte Deutscher Widerstand
German Resistance Memorial Center

4. Mai 2006 Zweifel. Gedenken als fettes Thema!? Verordnetes Gedenken? – Man kann Trauer und Erinnerung nicht auswählen. Was wäre, wenn die „Rote Kapelle", wenn der Widerstand gegen Hitler Erfolg gehabt hätte?

May 4, 2006 Doubt. Commemoration as a juicy topic!? Regulated thinking?— One cannot choose mourning and remembrance. What if the "Red Orchestra," what if the resistance against Hitler had been successful?

23. Mai 2006 Projektwoche „Als ich den ersten Blick in das Innere des aus zwei Räumen bestehenden Gebäudes geworfen hatte, dachte ich: Das war's? Nicht, dass ich etwas erwartet hätte, aber ich glaube, dass meine Augen etwas Anderes sehen wollen. Der Raum ist leerer, als ich gedacht habe. Zu viel Platz, um sich auszumalen, wie es einmal gewesen ist." Laura Heurich

May 23, 2006 Project Week "When I first looked inside the building, which contained two rooms, I thought, 'Was that it?' Not that I had expected anything, but I think my eyes wanted to see something different. The space is emptier than I thought. Too much space to be able to imagine how it was back then." Laura Heurich

In memoriam Mildred Harnack-Fish

... zur kleinsten Schar / ...with a chosen few

Gedenkstätte Deutscher Widerstand
German Resistance Memorial Center

... es mag sein, dass, frei nach Bertolt Brecht, die Schere aus dem Chaos eine Gestalt macht. Nicht aus Bequemlichkeit, sondern weil manche Formulierungen eher unbeholfen klingen, möchte ich sie nicht verändern. Ich denke, dass die von mir geschilderte Demut es verbietet, geglättete Aussagen über mein Vorhaben zu machen.

...it could be — to paraphrase Bertolt Brecht — that the scissors makes a figure out of the chaos. Although some formulations sound rather clumsy, it is not for convenience that I don't want to change them. I think the humility I have described prohibits me from making polished statements about my project.

29. Mai–2. Juni 2006 Probe aufs Exempel: Projektwoche
an der Mildred-Harnack-Oberschule in Berlin-Lichtenberg

May 29–June 2, 2006 Putting it to the test: Project Week at the
Mildred Harnack High School in Berlin-Lichtenberg

In memoriam Mildred Harnack-Fish

Gedenkstätte Deutscher Widerstand
German Resistance Memorial Center

Verscharren sollen sie auch meine Asche,
unwissend, dass auch ich,
meine Seele,
meine Ideale
in den Köpfen weiter leben.

Jessica Henschel

> They should bury my ashes in a shallow grave as well
> unaware that I, too,
> my soul
> my ideals
> live on in people's minds.
>
> Jessica Henschel

Berlin-Plötzensee, 10. September 2006 Gedenkmauer in der ehemaligen Hinrichtungsstätte mit Blick auf den Wasserturm und das Heizkraftwerk der Justizvollzugsanstalt Plötzensee

Berlin-Plötzensee, September 10, 2006 Memorial wall in the former place of execution, with a view of the water tower and the power station of Plötzensee Prison

Warum sie diese Goethe-Gedichte übersetzt hat ... es ist mir immer noch ein Rätsel!

Ein Gespräch von Yvonne Leonard mit Franz Rudolf Knubel

Yvonne Leonard Mehr als 60 Jahre nach der Ermordung von Mildred Harnack-Fish in Plötzensee widmest Du Dich ihr noch einmal in Deiner Arbeit *... zur kleinsten Schar/... with a chosen few. In memoriam Mildred Harnack-Fish.* Der deutsche Widerstand ist momentan wieder in das Blickfeld der Erinnerungskultur gerückt. Man kann in diesem Zusammenhang sicher von einer erneuten Revision der Erinnerungsbilder sprechen. Was waren Deine ganz persönlichen Gründe, eine Arbeit über den deutschen Widerstand zu machen? Es liegt ja nicht unbedingt auf der Hand, wenn man Deine künstlerische Biografie genau betrachtet.

Franz Rudolf Knubel Es gibt drei ganz unterschiedliche Anlässe, die mich auf dieses Projekt gebracht haben. 2004 habe ich in der California State University, Long Beach, und in der University of Washington, Tacoma, den Zyklus *Ground Zero, World Trade Center—New York City* über den 11. September 2001 gezeigt. Als die Arbeiten im Dezember 2004 wieder in Europa waren, sah ich dieses als Chance, etwas ganz Neues und Anderes zu machen. Ich habe mich hingesetzt und mir überlegt: Was ist eigentlich in Deinem eigenen Leben an historisch wichtigen Ereignissen passiert? Und nach längeren Überlegungen tauchte der 20. Juli, der Widerstand gegen Hitler auf. Dazu kam, dass mich das Center of European Studies in Kalifornien im Jahr 2005 gebeten hatte, eine künstlerische Übung mit den Studenten zum Thema „Ästhetik

Why did she translate those Goethe poems? ... it's still a mystery to me!

Yvonne Leonard interviews Franz Rudolf Knubel

Yvonne Leonard More than 60 years since Mildred Harnack-Fish was murdered in Plötzensee, you honor her once again in your work, *... zur kleinsten Schar/... with a chosen few. In memoriam Mildred Harnack-Fish.* The German resistance is currently a subject of revived interest in terms of historical remembrance. We can definitely speak of a new approach at the moment to images of remembrance. What were your very personal reasons for creating a work of art about the German resistance? After all, if we look at your biography as an artist, it's not obvious.

Franz Rudolf Knubel There are three different reasons that led to my taking up this project. In 2004 I showed a cycle, *Ground Zero, World Trade Center— New York City* about September 11, 2001, at California State University, Long Beach, and at the University of Washington, Tacoma. When the works were back in Europe in December 2004, I saw this as an opportunity to do something entirely new and different. I sat down and thought, "What has actually happened in your life in terms of important historical events?" And after thinking deeply, I came up with July 20th, 1944, the date that marks the resistance against Hitler. Secondly, in 2005 the Center of European Studies in California invited me to do an art exercise with the students on the topic, "Aesthetics in Resistance." So it was a short step to choosing the German resistance,

Franz Rudolf Knubel

des Widerstands" zu machen. Also lag es nahe, den deutschen Widerstand, den Widerstand gegen Hitler zu meinem Thema zu machen. Zum dritten habe ich auf Hiddensee Sabine Reichwein, die Tochter von Adolf Reichwein, der 1944 in Plötzensee hingerichtet wurde, kennen gelernt und einen Vortrag über ihren Vater gehört. So kam es, dass ich mich mit der Thematik immer mehr beschäftigte, anfing zu recherchieren und mich auf die Suche zu begeben.

Gab es darüber hinaus auch biografische Gründe, die in Deiner eigenen Lebensgeschichte eingelagert sind?

Ja, eine Geschichte, die mit meiner Großmutter Clara zusammenhängt. Sie hatte in der Veranda, wo sie in einer ziemlich stattlichen Art und Weise immer thronte und in der sie mich auch immer empfing, ein Bild hängen, ein ehemaliges Glasfenster aus der alten Dorfkirche, und darüber stand: „Sancta Clara". Sie war eine tiefgläubige Frau, die alles, was mit dem Nationalsozialismus zu tun hatte, aus tiefstem Herzen verabscheute und ablehnte. Daraus machte sie auch überhaupt keinen Hehl. Am 21. Juli 1944 hat sie einen Großteil ihrer Enkelkinder, ihrer Bediensteten und ihrer Kinder im Garten versammelt, sie selbst stand im Haus, hatte das Fenster geöffnet und hat sich an uns gewandt und gesagt: „Gestern ist ein großes Unglück passiert, ein Attentat auf Adolf Hitler, durchgeführt durch den Obersten Graf Stauffenberg, ist misslungen. Er lebt und es wird schrecklichere Zeiten geben als jetzt und wir müssen zusammenhalten." Diese Sätze sind mir nie aus dem Kopf gegangen.

Deine künstlerische Sozialisation hat ja in der Zeit der Studentenbewegung stattgefunden. Eine der zentralen Fragen dieser Zeit war die nach Auschwitz, nach den Verwicklungen der Vätergeneration in den Mord an 6 Millionen Juden, nicht die nach dem deutschen Widerstand.

the resistance against Hitler, as my topic. A third point is that on the island of Hiddensee I met Sabine Reichwein, the daughter of Adolf Reichwein, who was executed in Plötzensee in 1944, and heard a lecture about her father. This meant I was thinking repeatedly about the theme, so I started researching and set off on the trail.

Were there also other, personal, reasons connected with events in your own life?

Yes, there's a story about my grandmother Clara. She had a picture hanging in the verandah where she always received me, sitting in state in a rather imposing way. It was a stained-glass window that had once been part of the old village church, and above it were the words, "Sancta Clara" — Saint Clara. She was a deeply religious woman and hated and rejected everything to do with National Socialism. She made absolutely no secret of it, either. On July 21, 1944 she assembled most of her grandchildren and her servants and children in the garden. Remaining indoors, she opened the window, turned to us and said, "Yesterday a dreadful disaster happened. Colonel Graf Stauffenberg tried to assassinate Hitler, but failed. Hitler is still alive and we are facing even more terrible times than now, and we have to stand together." I have never forgotten what she said.

Your socialization as an artist happened at the time of the student movement. One of the key questions back then was about Auschwitz, about the complicity of the previous generation in the murder of 6 million Jews. It wasn't about the German resistance.

Looking back to that time, I was a student delegate from the Catholic Community in Tübingen, and the student delegate from the Protestant Student Community and I agreed to organize a joint screening of Alain Resnais' film *Night and Fog*. We showed it in the theater in Tübingen.

In memoriam Mildred Harnack-Fish

Gedenkstätte Deutscher Widerstand
German Resistance Memorial Center

Ja, wenn Du auf die Zeit zurückgreifst. Ich war Studentenvertreter der Katholischen Gemeinde in Tübingen und ich habe mit dem Vertreter der Evangelischen Studentengemeinde eine Abmachung getroffen, dass wir den Film *Nacht und Nebel* von Alain Resnais gemeinsam mit der Studentenvertretung zeigen, und das haben wir im Theater in Tübingen gemacht. Das hat auf mich einen sehr entscheidenden Eindruck gemacht. Alles andere war Schulweisheit. Es war eine sprachlose Zeit. Allerdings hatte ich in der Schule schon ein paar sehr prägende Eindrücke, denn wir haben Eugen Kogons *Der SS-Staat* gelesen, damals eher eine Ausnahme. Aber irgendwie hatten wir keinerlei Vorstellung. Bis ich 1960 bei der Bundeswehr war, auf einem Truppenübungsplatz in Bergen-Belsen, und wir geschlossen als eine Kompanie das Konzentrationslager besucht haben. Ich denke mal, das war mit 22 Jahren auf jeden Fall meine erste Berührung mit einem Ort gezielter jüdischer Vernichtung.

Und der deutsche Widerstand? War er auch ein Thema in diesem Zusammenhang oder wurde er mehrheitlich ausgeblendet?

Als ich 1961 zum Sommersemester nach Berlin kam, war das erste, was ich machte, soweit ich mich erinnere, dass ich nach Plötzensee ging. Otto Herbert Hajek hatte damals einen Kreuzweg in der Kirche Maria Regina Martyrum unmittelbar in der Nähe der Hinrichtungsstätte Plötzensee gebaut, der mich in seiner ganzen Neuigkeit sehr beeinflusste und tief beeindruckte. Jahre später, als ich mir die Arbeit noch einmal angesehen habe, hat er mich gar nicht mehr angerührt. Wahrscheinlich kommt einem heute diese Sprache eher abgenutzt vor. Das liegt natürlich auch daran, dass man selber so viel gesehen und gearbeitet hat.

That made a very decisive impression on me. Everything else I learnt came from books. It was a time when people didn't speak out. But at school I gained a few very important insights, because we read Eugen Kogon's book, *The SS State*, which was rather exceptional back then. Still, we didn't really have any idea — until 1960, when I was doing military service in the German Army. We were at a target practice ground in Bergen-Belsen, and we all visited the concentration camp together as a company. I was 22, and I think that was definitely my first contact with a place where Jews were deliberately exterminated.

What about the German resistance? Was it also a topic that came up in this context, or was it generally ignored?

When I went to Berlin for the summer semester in 1961, as far as I remember, the first thing I did was to go to Plötzensee. Back then, Otto Herbert Hajek had constructed a way of the cross in the church of Maria Regina Martyrum very close to the execution site at Plötzensee. His work seemed totally innovative — it had a great influence and made a profound impression on me. Years later, when I saw it again, it didn't affect me at all, because that kind of artistic language actually seems rather outworn now. Of course, this is also due to the fact that one has personally seen and worked so much.

Mildred Harnack-Fish tends to play a secondary role in the way people view the German resistance. How did she become the key person in your work? Or was it just by chance?

No, it wasn't by chance. My research began by concentrating on Peter Graf Yorck von Wartenburg and Helmuth James Graf von Moltke. I looked at written testimonies and their literary legacies. As an artist, I have to look at the material people have left behind, especially in

Mildred Harnack-Fish spielte ja in der Rezeption des deutschen Widerstandes eher eine Nebenrolle. Wie wurde sie zur zentralen Person Deiner Arbeit? Oder war das eher ein Zufall?

Nein, es war kein Zufall. Auf meiner Suche beschäftigte ich mich anfangs mit Peter Graf Yorck von Wartenburg und Helmuth James Graf von Moltke. Ich habe mir schriftliche Zeugnisse, Hinterlassenschaften von ihnen angeguckt. Als bildender Künstler muss ich mir ansehen, was von dem Material, das als Hinterlassenschaft vorhanden ist, vor allem verwertbar ist. Und dabei stieß ich auf die letzten Äußerungen, auf die letzten Briefe, die natürlich eine besondere Anmutung, eine Tiefe oder Trauer auszeichnete und die bei mir ein tiefes Mitleid ausgelöst haben. Bei dieser Gelegenheit ist mir dann auf Empfehlung von Dr. Tuchel in der Gedenkstätte Deutscher Widerstand das Buch *Mildred Harnack und die Rote Kapelle* von Shareen Blair Brysac empfohlen worden. Nachdem ich dieses Buch gelesen hatte, war ich mir sicher, dass dies meine Person wäre.

Aber Deine Recherchen gingen ja sicher weiter. Wo gab es den besonderen Moment der künstlerischen Annäherung an ihre Person?

Der Auslöser waren ihre Übersetzungen der Goethe-Gedichte in ihren letzten Lebenswochen. Das sind acht Gedichte. Auffällig war für mich die Schrift. Und zwar dieses Verfahren, dass sie mangels Papier in einer Ausgabe, die man ihr überlassen hatte, diese acht Gedichte zum großen Teil ganz, einige nur teilweise übersetzt hat, indem sie ihre eigene Übersetzung in die Texte mit Bleistift hineinschrieb. Diese Handschrift war für mich der Aufhänger, um daraus eine Möglichkeit der Näherung an ihre Person zu finden. Ich fand das so auffällig als Hinterlassenschaft.

terms of what can be used. In the process I stumbled on their last statements and final letters, and of course they expressed a particular charm, a depth or sadness that aroused deep empathy in me. This prompted Dr. Tuchel, the head of the German Resistance Memorial Center, to recommend the book *Resisting Hitler: Mildred Harnack and the Red Orchestra* by Shareen Blair Brysac. After reading it, I was sure that Mildred Harnack was the person for me.

But of course your research went further. At what point did you feel that you as an artist were getting close to her as a person?

I was inspired by her translations of Goethe's poems in the last weeks of her life. There are eight poems. I was struck by her handwriting: because she had no paper, she penciled her own translation into the printed text of the edition that she was allowed to keep with her. Most of the eight poems were completely translated, some only partly. I used her handwriting to find a way of approaching her as a person. I found it very striking as a legacy.

And while I was studying her translations, I started copying the Goethe poems again and again. It was part of my work at the university — after all, I have been teaching calligraphy for over 30 years. Then I transposed the English texts, her translations, into calligraphic form. For me, this was a meditative approach and an exercise at the same time. I had the feeling that I had got close to her as a person in a very appropriate way. She must have actually had a motivation for that — a reason for translating those poems by Goethe in the final days before her execution. It is still a mystery to me.

In memoriam Mildred Harnack-Fish

Gedenkstätte Deutscher Widerstand
German Resistance Memorial Center

Und bei der Beschäftigung mit ihren Übersetzungen habe ich begonnen, die Goethe-Gedichte nachzuschreiben, wieder und immer wieder. Es war ja ein Teil meiner Arbeit in der Universität, ich habe über 30 Jahre lang Schriftunterricht gegeben. Dann habe ich die englischen Texte, ihre Übersetzungen, in kalligrafischer Form übertragen. Das war für mich eine meditative Näherung und gleichzeitig auch eine Übung. Ich hatte das Gefühl, dass ich mich ihrer Person auf eine sehr adäquate Weise genähert habe. Sie musste ja ein Motiv gehabt haben, warum sie das gemacht hat. Warum sie diese Goethe-Gedichte übersetzt hat in den letzten Tagen vor ihrer Hinrichtung. Es ist mir immer noch ein Rätsel.

Gab es Zweifel, Probleme oder schier unlösbare Schwierigkeiten?

Ja natürlich. Die Auseinandersetzung mit Johannes Tuchel war in der ganzen Geschichte ungeheuer wichtig. Er hat nicht losgelassen. Ich bin mehrfach zu ihm gegangen, hab gesagt: „Ich bin verzweifelt, was die Arbeit betrifft, ich komme nicht weiter." Daraufhin sagte er: „Dann sind Sie auf dem besten Wege." Ich fand die Art und Weise, wie er mich immer wieder auf meine eigenen Mittel zurückgewiesen hat, eine ständige Herausforderung. Er sagte einfach: „Sie schreiben doch, Sie schreiben doch, warum schreiben Sie nicht? Es ist doch alles da." Das hat mich dann sehr bewegt, weil er noch sagte: „Je verzweifelter Sie sind, desto mehr zeigt es, dass Sie an der Sache sehr interessiert sind und dass Sie das tief betrifft."

Ging über die Schrift hinaus auch eine gewisse Faszination von der Person Mildred Harnack-Fish aus?

Mich haben natürlich auch die Schilderungen, vor allem von Harald Poelchau, dem Pfarrer in Plötzensee, über Mildred Harnack-Fish sehr angerührt. Sie hatte ja mehrere Leben: das

Did you have any doubts, difficulties or absolutely insoluble problems?

Yes, of course. My discussions with Johannes Tuchel were incredibly important throughout this process. He didn't let up. I went to him several times and said, "I'm desperate about the work, it's not going anywhere." He replied, "Then you're actually on the right track." I found the way he repeatedly sent me back to my own means of expression was a constant challenge. He simply said, "After all, you write, you write, why aren't you writing? Everything is actually there." This really affected me, because he also said, "The more desperate you are, the more it shows how deeply involved you are in this issue and how deeply it affects you."

Aside from the handwriting, did you feel fascinated in some way by Mildred Harnack-Fish's personality?

I was very moved, of course, by the descriptions of Mildred Harnack-Fish, especially by Harald Poelchau, the chaplain at Plötzensee. She had several lives: as a student and teacher at the university in Madison in the USA, and then as a teacher at the university in Berlin and as Arvid Harnack's wife. In fact, she had a high social status. She worked as an editor for Rütten & Loening and as a translator for two publishing houses, Fischer and Universitas. She acted as a hostess for Thomas Wolfe and for state visitors and diplomats, and was chairwoman of the American Women's Club in Berlin. In other words, I was interested in her personality both in terms of her inmost thoughts and the whole aspect of her role in society. What's more, she must have been beautiful and very charming. Arvid Harnack fell for her beauty at first sight. He went to the wrong lecture and landed up just by chance in the lecture room where she was — and then stayed sitting there. Forever, in a way. I was really fascinated by that.

Franz Rudolf Knubel

als Studentin und Lehrerin an der Universität Wisconsin in Madison in den USA, dann als Lehrerin an der Universität in Berlin und als Ehefrau von Arvid Harnack, und zwar schon sehr herausgehoben im gesellschaftlichen Leben. Sie arbeitete als Lektorin für Rütten & Loening und als Übersetzerin für den Fischer und den Universitas Verlag, betreute Thomas Wolfe, Staatsgäste und Diplomaten und war Vorsitzende des *American Womens Club* hier in Berlin. Also, die Person hat mich auf der einen Seite wegen ihrer Innigkeit, auf der anderen Seite in ihrer ganzen gesellschaftlichen Dimension interessiert. Und außerdem muss sie sehr anmutig und schön gewesen sein. Arvid Harnack ist ihrer Schönheit auf den ersten Blick erlegen. Er hatte sich ja in der Vorlesung vertan und ist nur durch Zufall in den Hörsaal gegangen, in dem sie war, und dann blieb er dort sitzen. Irgendwie für immer. Das hat mich schon fasziniert.

Du dokumentierst aber in Deinen Fotos die Gegenwart. Lapidar festgehalten, eine Jetztzeit der spurenlosen Vergangenheit. Verstehst du Deine Arbeit auch als eine Intervention in die Faktizität der Gedenkstätte, die ja sehr auf historische Dokumente konzentriert ist?

Natürlich arbeite ich als Künstler vollkommen anders. Ich gehe anders an die Sache ran. Allein die Fotos. Sie dokumentieren immer die Biografien oder die Lebensumgebungen. Das sehe ich jetzt auch bei der Biografie über Helmuth James Graf von Moltke von Günter Brakelmann, die gerade neu herausgekommen ist. Diese Fotos flankieren den Umgang mit Kindern, mit seiner Frau sowie seine soziale Umgebung und seine Arbeitsumgebung.

Ich hatte von Anfang an das Gefühl, ich muss etwas finden, damit ich die Gewissheit habe, hier hat Mildred Harnack gewohnt, hier hat sie gelebt. An keinem Ort, von dem ich wusste, den ich aufgesucht habe, wird ihrer gedacht, außer am Haus in der Hasenheide 61, wo sie zeitweise

But in your photos you document the present — captured tersely, a contemporary rendering of the past that has vanished without a trace. Do you also see your work as an intervention in the factual nature of the Memorial Center, which concentrates mostly on historical documents?

As an artist, I approach the subject differently. You only have to look at photos: they always document the life stories of the persons, or their surroundings. I can see that right now in Günter Brakelmann's biography of Helmuth James Graf von Moltke, which was published recently. These photos illustrate the way he was with children, with his wife and in his social and work environment. From the start there was the feeling I had to find something so that I could be sure about where Mildred Harnack had lived, to know where she had spent parts of her life.

I visited all the places I knew of, but there was none where she was commemorated except for the house at Hasenheide 61 where she lived for a while. I looked at the sidewalk there and said, "She must have set foot here." That was important for me. That's why I tried to create an analogy between a photo and a death mask. Death masks have something to do with physical contact, and this contact was particularly important to me. My quest for the places where she lived and worked was equally important — it was also a form of contact. This gave rise to a kind of topography in my mind as well. In approach, my work and the whole exhibition is more or less a depiction of the topography of commemoration in Berlin. And then I moved beyond the boundaries and went to Lithuania.

In memoriam Mildred Harnack-Fish

Gedenkstätte Deutscher Widerstand
German Resistance Memorial Center

gewohnt hat. Daraufhin habe ich die Steine angeschaut und gesagt: „Hier muss sie ihren Fuß draufgesetzt haben." Das war mir wichtig. Und deswegen habe ich versucht, eine Analogie zwischen einem Foto und einer Totenmaske herzustellen. Die Totenmaske hat ja etwas mit Berührung zu tun. Diese Berührung war mir besonders wichtig. Meine Suche nach den Orten, an denen sie gelebt und gearbeitet hat, war genauso wichtig. Auch eine Form der Berührung. Dadurch entstand eine Art Topografie, auch in meinem Kopf. Und mehr oder weniger ist meine Arbeit und die gesamte Ausstellung vom Ansatz her eine Abbildung der Topografie des Gedächtnisses hier in Berlin. Und dann habe ich die Grenzen überschritten und bin nach Litauen gefahren.

Eine Topografie des Gedächtnisses, in der das Vergessen die Erinnerung überlagert?

Ich versuche ja, das Vergessen wieder ins Gedächtnis zu kriegen. Diese Orte sind einfach alle Orte des Nichtgedenkens. Und dadurch, dass ich sie alle aufgesucht und dokumentiert habe, entstand eine neue Topografie als eine Art Leidensweg. In Preil (Preila), in Litauen ist sie verhaftet worden und der Fußboden der Gedenkstätte, das heißt, des so genannten Schuppens, wo die Hinrichtungen stattgefunden haben, ist der Endpunkt. Er ist auch der Kern der gesamten Arbeit, der Betonfußboden in Plötzensee.

Du denkst ihre Biografie in Deiner Arbeit also eigentlich vom Tod, von der Hinrichtung aus?

Ja, ich denke ihre Biografie eigentlich von hier aus zurück. Ich rolle das Leben dieser Frau von hinten auf und zwar von dieser eindrücklichen Situation, wie sie vor dem Schafott stehend gesagt habe: „... und ich habe Deutschland so geliebt." Vor etwa einem Jahr habe ich in der

A topography of commemoration in which forgetting overlays remembrance?

What I am really trying to do is to bring forgetting back into memory. All these sites are simply sites of non-remembrance. And the fact I went to see them all and documented them gave rise to a new topography as a kind of way of the cross. She was arrested in Preil (Preila) in Lithuania, and the floor of the memorial center, that is, of the so-called shed where they carried out the executions, is the last station. That concrete floor in Plötzensee is also the crux of the whole work.

So in this work you actually envisage her biography starting from her death, from the execution?

Yes, I actually trace her biography back from that point. I unfurl the life of this woman from back to front, in fact, from the momentous situation where she stood before the scaffold and is supposed to have said, "...and I have loved Germany so much." Around a year ago I saw a production of Schiller's *Maria Stuart* at the Schaubühne Theater in Berlin, and it occurred to me afterwards that the woman's whole life, as Schiller depicts it, is the path to the scaffold.

The meaning of location and time plays a special role in your work as a whole. Here, in relation to Mildred Harnack-Fish, you speak of the hell in which space and time converge.

In that context I can also mention a text I wrote immediately after my first attempt to make seven rubbings in Plötzensee. I had the feeling that the stillness in the room somehow basically represented all the 3,000 people who were executed there. At the same time, the stillness was the sum total of all the lamentations, all the fear that was experienced in

Berliner Schaubühne eine Aufführung von Schillers *Maria Stuart* gesehen und dabei ist mir im Nachhinein aufgefallen, dass das ganze Leben dieser Frau, so wie Schiller es darstellt, der Weg zum Schafott ist.

Die Bedeutung des Ortes und der Zeit spielt in Deinem Œuvre ja eine besondere Rolle. Hier, im Zusammenhang mit Mildred Harnack-Fish sprichst Du von der Hölle, in der sich Raum und Zeit verdichten.

In dem Zusammenhang kann ich ja auch auf einen Text hinweisen, den ich unmittelbar nach dem ersten Versuch in Plötzensee, Abreibungen zu machen, geschrieben habe. Da habe ich das Gefühl gehabt, dass diese Stille, die im Raum war, im Grunde alle 3 000 Hingerichteten in irgendeiner Weise repräsentierte. Die Stille war gleichzeitig die Summe aller Klagen, aller Angst, die dort an dem Ort in irgendeiner Weise gelebt wurde. Und darum habe ich ja auch diese Erinnerung an die Zeit der Arbeit, meiner ersten Session, wenn man so will, dort als Gang durch die Hölle bezeichnet. Das ist natürlich nur eine Metapher. Aber mit der bin ich als katholischer Christ ja auch aufgewachsen. Mit dieser Dialektik zwischen Himmel und Hölle, der Hölle als dem Ort der Strafe und zwar der immerwährenden Strafe. Ich glaube, dieses Immerwährende hängt diesem Ort an. Dass dieser Ort Besucher sofort dazu veranlasst, die Stimme zu senken, und ein verändertes Alltagsverhalten provoziert. Ich habe Leute gesehen, die dort hingekommen sind und sofort geistliche Lieder gesungen haben.

Nun ist diese Arbeit ja für die Gedenkstätte Deutscher Widerstand entstanden. Ein Ort, in dem Geschichten eher rekonstruiert werden. Dein Verfahren ist aber ein ganz anderes.

a way there, at that spot. And that is also why I have described my memory of the time I worked there, my first session if you like, as a passage through hell. Of course it's only a metaphor; but in fact, it's what I grew up with as a Catholic — with this dialectic between heaven and hell, with hell as the place of punishment, indeed, eternal punishment. I believe this eternal nature clings to that place, that it causes visitors to lower their voices immediately and provokes them to alter their everyday behavior. I've seen people who come in and start singing spiritual songs right away.

And now you have created this work for the German Resistance Memorial Center, a place where the emphasis is rather on reconstructing history. But you used a quite different method.

Contrary to all the scholarly advice I was given, I've always simply looked for ways out. For instance, I've documented and photographed all the places where the family or the couple Mildred and Arvid Harnack lived. This documentation finally ended in Plötzensee. But there I realized that I actually had to achieve a more intensive level of contact in relation to the moldings or rubbings. In fact, this is a very unique process. You have to kneel down while you are doing it. It's a very humble process; using all your physical strength, you go on your knees and, like an archaeologist, get close to the traces of the last minutes of life, and to death. You want to absorb them once again very concretely. And of course, the time you want to record with your rubbing has long since been overlaid.

Your work consists of three parts: the photographs of the places, the calligraphy and the rubbings, which actually form the heart of it.

In memoriam Mildred Harnack-Fish

... zur kleinsten Schar / ...with a chosen few

Gedenkstätte Deutscher Widerstand
German Resistance Memorial Center

Ich habe einfach, übrigens konträr zu allen Empfehlungen, die von Wissenschaftlern gekommen sind, immer Auswege gesucht. Unter anderem habe ich sämtliche Orte dokumentiert und fotografiert, an denen die Familie bzw. das Paar Mildred und Arvid Harnack gelebt hat. Das Dokumentieren endet ja letztlich in Plötzensee. Aber eigentlich ist mir an dieser Stelle klar geworden, dass es wohl eine intensivere Stufe der Näherung geben müsse, was ja dann die Abformungen beziehungsweise die Abreibungen betrifft. Das ist ja ein sehr eigenartiger Vorgang. Du musst Dich ja dabei hinknien. Ein sehr demütiger Vorgang, mit aller Kraft des Körpers, näherst Du Dich auf den Knien wie ein Archäologe den Spuren der letzten Lebensminuten und des Todes. Ganz konkret willst Du sie noch einmal abnehmen. Und natürlich ist die Zeit, die Du abreiben willst, längst darüber abgelagert.

Deine Arbeit besteht ja aus drei Teilen, neben den Fotografien der Orte die kalligrafische Arbeit und die Frottagen, die eigentlich doch das Zentrum bilden.

Ich habe in den Frottagen, und zwar in dem Moment, wo ich die sieben Abreibungen unter dem Galgen gemacht habe, das Gefühl gehabt, das ist der Kern der Ausstellung und nicht meine Schreibübung. Ich habe die kalligrafischen Übertragungen und die fotografische Dokumentation der Orte eher als Exerzitien empfunden. Diese Frottagen, die ja eine Art von Näherung, ja Berührung mit dem ganz Konkreten sind, haben auch mit einer großen Art von Submission zu tun. Wenn Du Dich hinkniest, unterwirfst Du Dich auch.

Von einer der Frottagen, der das ganze Grauen einbeschrieben ist, gibt es auch einen Abguss, der jetzt als Denkmal an der Mildred-Harnack-Oberschule in Berlin steht.

While doing the rubbings I had the feeling—at the very moment, in fact, when I made the rubbings under the gallows—that this is the crux of the exhibition, rather than my calligraphic exercises. I felt that the calligraphic transpositions and the documentary photographs of the places were more like a religious exercise. These rubbings, which are actually like an approximation, like close contact with the very concrete situation, are connected with a kind of deep submission. When you kneel down, it is like a kind of submission, in fact.

One of the rubbings is imbued with the whole horror. There is also a metal cast of it that now stands as a monument at the Mildred Harnack High School in Berlin.

While this whole work was in progress, I was unexpectedly commissioned to make the memorial plaque. At first I felt overwhelmed by this, and I must say that ever since I studied classical drama I kept remembering a formula—the unity of space, time, and action. But I had to realize time and again that the formula can't necessarily be translated into our contemporary way of thinking. Instead, I have the impression that reality, as Robert Delaunay once said, represents a broken mirror to us. We always see just fragments, not the whole picture.

The solution for the memorial plaque occurred to me through the rubbings—that is, to capture the site of the killing. There is a report that in 1943 an air raid partly destroyed the execution shed and put the guillotine out of action. Apparently it was wrenched out of its socket in the floor. On the plaque, I think the place is evident first of all, and then the time. I mean place and time in the sense that I write on it when the killing took place, and the action, the deed or attitude to life, converges on the words, "…and I have loved Germany so much." In retrospect— and this was not intentional— this harmony of place, time and action became clear to me, and it is not a broken mirror in which we perceive the reality of that period, it all converges.

In diese ganze Arbeit ist ja unerwarteter Weise der Auftrag gekommen, diese Gedenkplatte zu gestalten. Das hat mich natürlich überfordert am Anfang und ich muss sagen, ich habe seit der Beschäftigung mit klassischen Dramen immer wieder diese eine Formel, die Einheit von Ort, Zeit und Handlung, im Kopf gehabt und habe immer wieder festgestellt, dass sich diese Formel auf die heutige Denkweise nicht unbedingt übertragen lässt. Ich habe eher den Eindruck, dass sich die Wirklichkeit, wie Robert Delaunay das mal gesagt hat, für uns wie ein zerschlagener Spiegel darstellt. Wir sehen immer nur Fragmente, aber nicht die Ganzheit.

Mir ist bei der Gelegenheit über die Abreibungen diese Lösung für die Gedenkplatte gekommen. Nämlich, dass ich den Ort der Tötung festhalten muss. Es gibt einen Bericht, dass 1943 ein Bombardement den Hinrichtungsschuppen teilweise zerstört und die Guillotine außer Kraft gesetzt hat. Sie ist offensichtlich aus den Halterungen im Boden gerissen worden. Ich finde, auf dieser Tafel stellt sich erst einmal der Ort dar, dann die Zeit. Ort, Zeit, indem ich hier aufschreibe, wann die Tötung stattgefunden hat, und die Handlung, diese Lebenshandlung oder -haltung verdichtet sich in dem „… und ich habe Deutschland so geliebt". Im Nachhinein ist mir eigentlich – das ist keine Absicht gewesen – diese Übereinkunft von Ort, Zeit und Handlung klar geworden und es ist eben kein zerbrochener Spiegel, in dem wir die Wirklichkeit dieser Zeit wahrnehmen, sondern sie ist verdichtet.

Das ist ja auch ein Prinzip Deiner Frottagen, eigentlich hat der Ort keinen Namen, sondern er erweitert sich zu einer eigenen Welt, gleichsam als Erkenntnis von Welt.

Ja, die Abreibung ist ja vor allem Erfahrung und das Experiment einer Beziehung. Sie geht über den Gegenstand hinaus. Nimmt man als Beispiel ein Foto von einer Hand und daneben den Abdruck, so zeigt sich das Authentische der Hand im Abdruck und geht zugleich darüber

That is also a principle of your rubbings—the place actually has no name, but it extends into a world of its own, and is a perception of the world at the same time.

Yes, a rubbing is primarily an experience and the experiment of a relationship. It goes beyond the object itself. For example, if you take a photo of a hand and put a print from the hand next to it, the print shows the authenticity of the hand and simultaneously transcends it. The same applies to Plötzensee as the site of killing, and the rubbings from the floor. Georges Didi-Huberman once said that the cast is a collision, a revelation, and a distortion all in one (Georges Didi-Huberman: *Ähnlichkeit und Berührung, Archäologie, Anachronismus und Modernität des Abdrucks*, Cologne 1999). It has an afterlife. That's what this place and the rubbings mean to me. For me, it's a really terrible place. The afterlife that Huberman speaks of can be seen in relief, in the fact one knows what it is. And then it extends into a world.

In his article, "Margins and Centers—the Journey of Exploration of the Artist Rudolf Knubel," Thomas Zaunschirm writes of your work, "He doesn't show what he knows. His research is rather a project in the service of recollection. Here he is entering in new territory, for which we still have no name." Is this the territory for which we still have no name?

It goes beyond death, beyond the murders, a place without a name. What constantly preoccupies me now, after the end of this work—when it has its form, for an exhibition always has something final about it—is the question of whether I will simply work on a new theme. The project is put away then, or can be laid aside; it can be packed into a crate. I don't know what I want to do. All the same, I'm thinking beyond this state. I think I can sleep better

In memoriam Mildred Harnack-Fish

... zur kleinsten Schar / ...with a chosen few

Gedenkstätte Deutscher Widerstand
German Resistance Memorial Center

Von Franz Rudolf Knubel gestaltete Gedenktafel im Hof der
Mildred-Harnack-Oberschule in Berlin-Lichtenberg, Februar 2007
Architektin: Marie-Luise Klein, Büro für Freiraumplanung, Berlin
Typografie: Gerd Fleischmann, Ulrichshusen
Bronzeguss: Gießerei Wolfgang Frische, Bedburg-Hau
Foto: Eckhard Jonalik, Berlin

Memorial plaque designed by Franz Rudolf Knubel in the courtyard
of Mildred Harnack High School in the Lichtenberg district, Berlin,
February 2007
Architect: Marie-Luise Klein, Büro für Freiraumplanung, Berlin
Typography: Gerd Fleischmann, Ulrichshusen
Bronze cast: Gießerei Wolfgang Frische, Bedburg-Hau
Photo: Eckhard Jonalik, Berlin

hinaus. So wie der Ort Plötzensee, der Ort der Tötung und die Abreibungen vom Fußboden. Georges Didi-Huberman (Georges Didi-Huberman: *Ähnlichkeit und Berührung. Archäologie, Anachronismus und Modernität des Abdrucks,* Köln 1999) hat einmal gesagt, dass der Abguss ein Zusammenprall ist, eine Enthüllung und Entstellung in einem. Er hat ein Nachleben. Und das sind für mich dieser Ort und die Abreibungen. Er ist für mich ein ganz furchtbarer Ort. Er hat das Nachleben, von dem Huberman spricht, in dem Relief, indem man weiß, was das ist. Und dann erweitert es sich zu einer Welt.

Thomas Zaunschirm schrieb in seinem Artikel "Margins and centers — the Journey of Exploration of the Artist Rudolf Knubel" über Deine Arbeiten: "He doesn't show what he knows. His research is rather a project in the service of recollection. Here he is entering in new territory, for which we still have no name." Ist es das Territorium, das noch keinen Namen hat?

Er geht über den Tod, über das Morden hinaus, ein Ort ohne Namen. Was mich derzeit immerzu beschäftigt: Werde ich nach dem Abschluss dieser Arbeit – dann hat sie ja ihre Gestalt, denn eine Ausstellung hat immer etwas Endgültiges – einfach ein neues Thema bearbeiten? Das Projekt ist dann abgelegt oder ablegbar, man kann es in eine Kiste packen. Ich weiß nicht, was ich tun will. Trotzdem denke ich über diesen Zustand schon hinaus. Ich denke, ich kann dann besser schlafen. Alle Bilder beschäftigen mich immer noch in meinen Träumen, auch in den letzten Tagen wieder. Die Lektüre der Biografie von Moltke als dem führenden Kopf des Kreisauer Kreises und Mildred Harnack als Ehefrau Arvid Harnacks, des führenden Kopfes in der Roten Kapelle. Ich habe gerade auf einer Reise durch Spanien Serien von verpackten Schieferplatten fotografiert. Dabei ist mir die Idee gekommen, das wäre ein gutes Motiv, um den deutschen Widerstand zu dokumentieren, indem man einfach 5 000 oder wie viele Menschen in diesem Zusammenhang hingerichtet wurden, 5 000 Platten nimmt und auf jede Platte den Namen

then. All the images still occupy my dreams, and yet again recently, reading the biographies of Moltke as the leading figure in the Kreisau Circle and Mildred Harnack as the wife of Arvid Harnack, the leading figure in the Red Orchestra. I've just been on a trip in Spain where I photographed series of packed slate tiles. That gave me the idea that a good motif for documenting the German resistance would be to take 5,000 tiles for the 5,000 or however many people who were executed and write each of their names on a tile — to actually document them for once, not just on paper. I have the feeling this is my mission, it's pushing me on beyond this present work. I think I can hardly find a greater convergence.

In memoriam Mildred Harnack-Fish

... **zur kleinsten Schar** /...with a chosen few

Gedenkstätte Deutscher Widerstand
German Resistance Memorial Center

schreibt. Damit sie wirklich einmal dokumentiert werden, außer auf Papier. Ich habe das Gefühl, dass es meine Aufgabe ist, es drängt mich, über diese Arbeit hinaus. Ich glaube, dass ich eigentlich keine größere Verdichtung finden kann.

Ich lebe nicht alleine, ich erinnere nicht alleine, ich fühle nicht alleine:

I do not live alone, I do not remember alone, I do not feel alone:

Clara Bauer, Sabine Reichwein, Cornelia Brüninghaus-Knubel, Johannes Tuchel, Susanne Brömel, Karl-Heinz Lehmann, Dagmar Schulz, Ute Kopp, Ellen Galizzi, Gerd Fleischmann, Maike Beyer, Stefan Bienk, Charlotte Securius-Carr, Richard Aker, Wolfgang Brandt, Hans Coppi, Hans Mommsen, Barbara Ischinger, Ilona Kalb, Ursula Renner-Henke, Ludger Claßen, Christina Reich, Rosemarie Neubauer, Margitta Unger, Verena Schulte-Fischedick, Andreas Friedlaender, Heike Köhler, Jennifer Barthel, Doreen Brieske, Josephina Franz, Admira Hasific, Franca Heiden, Jessica Henschel, Laura Heurich, Anna Petrov, Viktor Rosenbach, Alexander Schaefer, Janine Seddig, Sarah Kienscherf, Julia Endemann, Melanie Zimmermann, Elena Hahn, Dustin Harnack, Martin Walker, Reiner Trost, Gertrud Markus, Kurt Metschies, Carsten Bolz, Marie-Luise Klein, Eberhard Wolff, Eitel Friedrich Scholz, Lotte Wolff, Susanne Henle, Gerhard R. Neipp, Doris Neipp, Lothar Zechlin, Thomas Zaunschirm, Andreas von Weizsäcker, Andreas Fischer, Ralf Richter, Wolfdietrich Jost und Corinna Eichhorn.

Franz Rudolf Knubel

1938	geboren in Münster (Westfalen)
1960–1966	Studium der Kunstgeschichte, Germanistik und Philosophie an der Universität Tübingen sowie der Kunst- und Werkerziehung an der Hochschule für Bildende Künste Berlin u. a. bei Ludwig Gabriel Schrieber, Fred Thieler und Walter Hess
1964–1968	Mitbegründer der Künstlergruppe Großgörschen 35, zusammen mit Eduard Franoszek, Karl Horst Hödicke, Reinhard Lange, Markus Lüpertz, Peter Sorge, Lambert Maria Wintersberger u. a.
seit 1968	Künstlerische Lehre
1970	Gründung der SYSTEM-DESIGN-Planungsgruppe für visuelle Leitsysteme Recklinghausen-Essen mit Bernd Damke und Eckart Heimendahl
1971–2004	Hochschullehrer an der Folkwangschule für Gestaltung Essen, Universität/Gesamthochschule Essen, Fachbereich Gestaltung-Kunsterziehung
1974	Gründung der Arbeitsgruppe Visuelle Leitsysteme – mit Stefan Lengyel u. a. für den Neubau der Universität/Gesamthochschule Essen
seit 1975	gemeinsame Arbeiten mit der Fotografin Ursula Schulz-Dornburg
1976–1977	Stipendiat der Villa Massimo, Deutsche Akademie Rom
1986–1987 und 2000	Lehrtätigkeit an der California State University Long Beach, Department of Romance, German, Russian Languages and Literatures, Kalifornien, USA, Stipendiat der Fulbright-Foundation in den Vereinigten Staaten von Amerika lebt in Essen

Publikationen (Auswahl)

Franz Rudolf Knubel: *Works on Paper, 1971–2004*. Mit Texten von Klaus Herding und Thomas Zaunschirm, Essen 2004

November 19, 1995 — Essen, Germany, Pioneer Pilot. In: Kent Kleinman; Leslie van Duzer (Eds.): *Rudolf Arnheim: Revealing vision*, Ann Arbor 1999

Franz Rudolf Knubel: *Périphéries et Centres. Voyages d'exploration visuelle 1971–97*. Text von Thomas Zaunschirm. Hrsg. vom Goethe-Institut, Rabat-Casablanca 1998

Franz Rudolf Knubel: *Spur der Kraniche – Tracing Cranes*. Forschungsprojekt der Universität/ Gesamthochschule Essen 1994/1997, Buchhandlung Walther König, Köln 1997

Franz Rudolf Knubel; Thomas Strauch; Jochen Ehlert; Ralf Wassermann: *Zu Besuch bei Rudolf Arnheim*. Video-Interview (Ann Arbor, USA) in Kooperation mit dem Medienzentrum der Universität/Gesamthochschule Essen 1994

Franz Rudolf Knubel; Thomas Strauch; Jochen Ehlert; Ralf Wassermann: *Steine und Sternenweg. Vier Schritte auf dem Weg nach Santiago de Compostela*. Videoessay, Essen 1993

Ute Lefarth (Hrsg.): *Franz Rudolf Knubel: Male, an denen die Sonne angebunden ist. Studien über den gradlinigen Schatten, das Gesetz der Stunde und anderes*. Skulpturen, Zeichnungen, Photographien, Marl 1990

Franz Rudolf Knubel; Wolfgang Pilz: KIT-Kiste, Koffer, Einheit. In: *Kunst lehren und lernen*. Hrsg. vom Funktionsbereich Kunst- und Designpädagogik im Fachbereich 4 der Universität/Gesamthochschule Essen, Essen 1986

Franz Rudolf Knubel (Hrsg.): *Die Jahreszeiten. Eine Systematik der Grundlagen der Gestaltung. Anleitung zur Entfaltung der Sinne und ihrer Handhabung*. Forschungsprojekt an der Universität/Gesamthochschule Essen 1981–1983, Essen 1984

Franz Rudolf Knubel; Ursula Schulz-Dornburg: *Der Tigris des alten Mesopotamien. Irak 1980*. Kestner Gesellschaft, Hannover 1981

Franz Rudolf Knubel; Ursula Schulz-Dornburg: *Ansichten von Pagan, Burma*, Köln 1978

Bernd Damke; Eckart Heimendahl; Franz Rudolf Knubel: *System Design*. Katalog Kunsthalle Düsseldorf und Museum Ulm, 1970

© 2007 by Gedenkstätte Deutscher Widerstand, Berlin;
   Franz Rudolf Knubel, Essen
Künstlerische Gesamtleitung   Artistic project director
   Franz Rudolf Knubel
Projektleitung und -koordination
Project direction and coordination
   Petra Behrens, Susanne Brömel, Dr. Johannes Tuchel
Texte der Ausstellungsfahnen   Exhibition texts
   Franz Rudolf Knubel, Yvonne Leonard, Dr. Johannes Tuchel
Biografische Dokumentation „Mildred Harnack-Fish"
Mildred Harnack-Fish — Biographical Documentation
   Konzeption und Texte   Concept and texts
      Petra Behrens
   Englische Redaktion und Koordination
   English editing and coordination
      Karen Margolis
   Englische Übersetzungen   English translation
      Allison Brown, Karen Margolis, Andre Simonoviescz,
      Katy Derbyshire, Sylvie Malich
   Gestaltung und Produktion   Design and production
      Karl-Heinz Lehmann
Redaktion Ausstellung, Katalog und Biografische Dokumentation
„Mildred Harnack-Fish"   Exhibition, catalogue and biographical
documentation on Mildred Harnack-Fish edited by
   Petra Behrens, Ute Stiepani
   Mitarbeit   Consultants
      Dr. Ekkehard Klausa, Taina Sivonen, Susanne Brömel
Englische Übersetzungen Ausstellung und Katalog
English translation of exhibition and catalogue
   Karen Margolis
Fotografie   Photographs
   Stefan Bienk, Laura Heurich, Eckhard Jonalik,
   Franz Rudolf Knubel, Heike Köhler
Ausstellungsgestaltung   Exhibition design
   Gerd Fleischmann
Herstellung der Ausstellungsfahnen   Exhibition banners made by
   Digitaler GROSSprint, Berlin
Technische Realisierung der Ausstellung   Technical organization
   Karl-Heinz Lehmann, Susanne Brömel
Katalog, Konzeption und Gestaltung   Catalogue design
   Gerd Fleischmann
   Umschlag   Cover illustration
      Franz Rudolf Knubel, *Berlin-Plötzensee, Hüttigpfad:
      Hinrichtungsstätte 3/7*, 2007 (Detail)
   Frontispiz   Frontispiece
      Mildred Harnack, ca. 1930
Gesamtherstellung   Printed by
   allprintmedia, Berlin

ISBN 978-3-926082-31-2